ENDORSEMENTS

He Said Yes

To answer in the affirmative. To stand in agreement. To give permission. Some of the reasons we would say yes. It is one of the most common words in our vocabulary, and sometimes the word we are most reluctant to say because yes is a commitment. To give our yes means there must be a follow through on our part. Yes is the lynchpin, the prerequisite, for partnership with God. God asks big questions that lead into big Kingdom purposes, but the launching into that partnership hinges on our yes.

Jason Abney has written a beautiful telling of life and death, experiences that taught him the incredible value and power of saying yes to Jesus. *He Said Yes: Why Your Yes Matters* is more than a worthy read. It is an essential read that will lead you to Biblical truths that validate your yes to God, encouraging you to answer Him in the affirmative, to stand with Him in agreement, and to give Him permission to partner with you in Kingdom purpose. *He Said Yes* is a blessed read!

— **Jeffery Davis**
Lead Pastor, Overflow Church

In *He Said Yes: Why Your Yes Matters*, Jason Abney invites readers into a transformative journey of saying yes to God. Through his personal story of a near-death experience and a face-to-face encounter with Jesus, Jason illustrates the profound impact one simple decision can have—not only on our earthly lives but on our eternal destinies and the lives of those around us. With vivid and descriptive storytelling, he takes us on a heavenly journey that feels so real, it's as if we are right there with him, witnessing the glory of God and the power of His love.

Jason's story is a powerful testament to the life-changing power of obedience to God. His encounter with Jesus wasn't just a spiritual experience—it was a call to action, an invitation to step into our true identity and inheritance as children of God. This book will build your faith, renew your hope, and equip you to walk in the fullness of what God has for you.

Over the years, I've had the honor of walking alongside Jason and witnessing firsthand the fruit of his yes. His obedience to God has not only transformed his life but has impacted an entire region. The evidence of his faithfulness is undeniable, and it serves as a reminder that if God can do incredible things through Jason's yes, He can do the same through ours.

This book will challenge you to embrace your own yes and inspire you to see how God can use your willingness to radically transform your life and the world around you.

— **Derrick M. Snodgrass, Jr., D.Min.**
Lead Pastor, Willow Church, Lake Jackson, TX

Jason Abney's book *He Said Yes: Why Your Yes Matters* shows us that God chose you, redeemed you, transformed you, and empowered you because your life and your yes matter to God and His Kingdom.

Every book of the Bible reveals God's majestic love and purpose for us, not just in eternity but right now. Scripture clearly teaches us that we are created in the image of God and called to manifest His life through the power of the Holy Spirit each day.

No matter where we are or what our surroundings may be, we carry the life of God in these earthly bodies and when we have given Him our yes, He will pour that love, life, and power into others. He longs to bring hope, strength, encouragement, and victory to people through your yes, from the church building to the workplace.

He doesn't wait till we graduate seminary. He will start immediately if we give Him our yes every day. The true-life stories of the Bible are the evidence that our yes matters and has the power to change lives and even cities.

In *He Said Yes: Why Your Yes Matters*, Pastor Jason Abney releases a very timely and powerful word to our generation. I encourage you to let it motivate and empower you to give God your yes.

— **Lance Johnson**
Founder, Lions Gate Ministry Training Center

He Said Yes is the story of one man's response to the Lord's call to follow Him closely. I have watched Jason Abney's life for several years. He is a man sold out to the will of God. Through his experience in these pages, you will discover practical help in hearing the voice of God and being used by Christ to make a positive impact on your world. It is one thing to be saved and bound for Heaven. It is another, to influence your world and to take as many with you as possible on the way.

If we are honest, most of us know something God wants us to do in the near or distant future. That fact alone demonstrates that the issue is not "hearing God." Rather, it is doing what we know He is asking of us. Saying yes and following through in obedience is where the action is.

My first yes came during a church camp. At 17 I knew God was asking me to change my career plans and enter vocational Christian service. One night I stepped out at a campfire and said "Yes!" Sixty years have passed since that moment and I have never regretted my decision. Through my yes, God has used my life to love and help many others find the way. This book will show you how to say yes and how to walk that out, keeping in step with the Holy Spirit. The potential impact of one yes is amazing!

— Steve Brown
Pastor Emeritus

Making a commitment to say yes, whatever the Lord asks you to do, is not just important but vital. Nothing miraculous ever happens on earth until someone says yes to the Lord. Everything follows a yes.

When I read Jason Abney's *He Said Yes: Why Your Yes Matters,* I recalled a time early in my ministry leading a team of missionaries to El Salvador.

While in El Salvador we worked during the day to build our local pastor a home and an extension of the church. We labored all day in the brutal heat while holding pastors and leaders conferences daily and nightly crusade events.

An open-air crusade was planned for the last evening. The wind was hurricane level, blowing dirt. Everyone was tired and ready to go home. Canceling the open-air crusade would be easy. We could still call the trip a huge success.

We held the meeting. Afterward, we prayed for those in attendance. They brought a deaf seven-year-old boy. I wept over the child and asked the Lord to heal him. I rebuked the deaf spirit and commanded his body to be healed. I told his mother standing behind him to say his name.

When she did, he turned his head and looked at his mother. The first words he ever heard were his own mother calling out his name. The boy looked stunned and amazed, the mother wept, I wept, and the crowd rejoiced!

This series of yeses lead to a seven-year-old deaf boy being miraculously healed.

What if I had said no to the trip? What if out of fatigue we had canceled the open-air meeting? What if we had let the weather change our yes to a no? While I did not heal that young man, my yes provided the pathway for the Lord to do a miracle for him!

I wonder what "seven-year-old boy" is linked to your yes. Learn more about your yes in *He Said Yes: Why Your Yes Matters.*

— David Edmondson
Pastor, Covenant Connections Church, Flowery Branch, GA

Pastor Jason Abney has provided the Church with a brilliant path for growing spiritually from "just saved and sedentary" to fully serving the Lord in *He Said Yes: Why Your Yes Matters.*

Jason has a mature Christian faith with operational, God-given gifts of the Holy Spirit, including discernment, prophecy, accurate visions, teaching, and forming disciples. He served faithfully in a local church, rising to lead deacons and teaching youth. *He Said Yes* chronicles his colorful early life, many interesting career experiences, and his dramatic death and coming back to life. He currently hosts an ongoing visitation of the Holy Spirit bringing healing and deliverance at his church Life Of Love Ministries in Martinsville, Indiana.

Jason transparently tells his life story in an engaging and encouraging way that invites everyone to join him on life's most exciting way to live in a joint venture with Jesus. Jason's presentation of his four pillars for a strong Christian life of love, identity, freedom, and encounter will be invaluable to the reader. I highly recommend He Said Yes for your best life now!

— Pastor Larry Arendas
Founder and President, Spirit and Truth Ministries
International

In *He Said Yes: Why Your Yes Matters*, Jason Abney tells of his yes in response to God's yes. When we give God our yes, the work begins. What you say yes to requires preparation, development, and training. The Lord asks us to partner with Him, to commit ourselves to prayer, study, and equipping. The Holy Spirit will do His part to make us ready, but we have a responsibility to cooperate with Him in our own development.

Part of Jason's yes was his involvement in Kineo Ministry Training Center. He aligned himself with a training program to equip him for what was ahead. He realized he needed depth in the Word and an understanding of his identity, his authority, and the covenant in Jesus. Kineo equipped Jason with a deeper knowledge of the Word of God, how to apply it, and teach others to walk in it.

As you embark on the journey your yes will bring, your feet must be planted in the Word of God to come through life's storms. Kineo Ministry Training Center helped prepare Jason to face any storm.

In giving your yes to Jesus, you can prepare at Kineo Ministry Training Center for training. The Kineo opportunity awaits you.

— Karen Smith, D. Min.
President, Kineo Ministry Training Center

Embedded within the pages of my good friend Jason Abney's book He Said Yes: Why Your Yes Matters, extracted from the very heart of the Father, are four words. No! Four pillars.

Love. Identity. Freedom. Encounter.

These four pillars have been erected on a foundational truth . . . God can do *any* and *all* things on His own, but He chooses not to.

From creation until Christ's return, the kingdom of Heaven extends a holy invitation to the "whosoevers" of humanity into a divine relationship with the King of Glory. Acceptance into this type of companionship grants each recipient immediate access to a promising path paved with precious adventure. All that is required from you is one word . . . yes!

I pray as you read the pages of this book, your heart swells and your eyes leak. I pray your soul catches fire and your hunger for the Lord becomes insatiable. Embrace and explore the full power of your yes, and all the amazing roads your yes can pave for you and the world around you.

Your yes has potential. Your yes has power. Discover it. Release it. Operate in it. Share it. Be bold in it. Roar with it. Go with it.

Ditch your limitations. Watch your yes be used as a key for the Lord to open brand new doors for you. May your yes lead you to new people, new places and new experiences. With everything in me, I encourage you with this final quote from Bob Goff. Bob said, "I used to think you had to be special for God to use you, but now I know you simply need to say yes."

— Marty Darracott
Executive Pastor, Christ Fellowship Church,
Dawsonville, GA

He Said Yes

Why Your Yes Matters

Jason L. Abney

Never Alone Publishing

Cover painting by Richard Tomas Railey at https://www.richardtomasimaging.com/shop

Edited and coached by Rachel Hills at https://authorswhoserve.com/

Published by Never Alone Publishing, Fort Wayne, IN 46825

ISBN: 979-8-9913590-3-0 (paperback)

979-8-9913590-4-7 (ebook)

Printed in USA

First Edition

DISCLAIMER

These stories are told as I remember them. Some names or details are changed to protect privacy. The truths I learned are genuine and universal but any factual errors are mine alone.

-Jason

CONTENTS

FOREWORDS

Jason Abney's book *He Said Yes* tells us *Why Your Yes Matters*. Your yes unlocks new doors, closes old ones, and prevents you from walking through the wrong doors. Not only does your yes affect you, it greatly impacts those closest to you.

The revival that came to our church in 2018 came as a result of a series of difficult yeses. Before the Lord allowed me to progress into the deeper realms of His glory, He required something from me—He wanted my yes. I couldn't experience what was next until I gave Him my no-strings-attached yes.

In *He Said Yes: Why Your Yes Matters*, Jason Abney invites you on a challenging journey—a journey that is a faith walk, filled with mystery and wild experiences.

Every new level in your life is preceded by a demand from the Lord and consequently a genuine yes on your end. Failure to give Him this yes stops your progress and spiritual development.

For example, when He asks you to tithe and you say yes, closed financial windows over your life now open.

When He asks you to forgive the person who harmed you and you say yes, you are released from a prison and the bitterness is uprooted.

When He asks you to share the gospel with your neighbor and you say yes, the neighbor hears the greatest news of all time and repents. Your yes changed his quality of life and eternity.

When the Lord asks you to cut the grass of a widow on your street and you say yes, you have not only blessed her, you changed her life.

I am learning that God is after my yes.

I have often wondered why the Lord said of King David, "… he is a man after my own heart." I found the answer in Acts 13:22. "David is a man after my heart because he will do all my will" or "all I ask him to do." Whatever God asked of him, he said, "I will do it."

In this timely book, Pastor Jason, who has given God his yes, does an excellent job of guiding you to the place of total surrender and complete compliance with God's ask. His individual story is compelling, unique, suspenseful, and heartwarming.

I challenge you to feel Pastor Jason's heart as he pleads with us—say yes to the One who is worthy.

— **Todd Smith, D.Min.**
Lead Pastor, Christ Fellowship Church, Dawsonville, GA
Host Pastor, North Georgia Revival

One of my favorite worship songs of recent years is "Jesus at the Center of it All." Jason Abney embodies that sense of perspective in his book *He Said Yes: Why Your Yes Matters*.

Following his time visiting heaven, saying yes was the first and best step Pastor Jason took in his life of Kingdom service. You can see it today in the way he and his wife, Pastor Shelly, lead a supernatural church.

His invitation to join our Lord in the waters of baptism demonstrates a hunger for the abiding, energizing ability of the Holy Spirit. This invitation comes from a man who knows the power of a yes!

Read his book *He Said Yes: Why Your Yes Matters*. It has the necessary information to release the anointing of the Holy Spirit who enables us to do the "greater works" of Jesus.

— **Roberts Liardon**
CEO, Roberts Liardon Ministries

1. VISITING HEAVEN

I don't recommend dying in a car wreck but it's how I
visited heaven the first time. On my way home from
work, I was driving through the green light of a four-lane
road at full speed. An older gentleman, who didn't see
his red arrow, turned left in front of me and bam. Lights
out.

I woke up in the ambulance long enough to hear
them say I had a broken arm, broken leg, and a
fractured skull.

Between the impact and waking in the ambulance, I
went to heaven.

Seeing Heaven

I stood in beautiful green grass, really tall and plush.
Every blade was soft but shaped like a sword. I saw
Jesus standing there. He wore blue jeans and a blue
plaid shirt. In this beautiful moment, I knew it was
Jesus.

My first thought was: Why are you wearing blue jeans and a blue plaid shirt? He seemed to hear my thoughts and answered aloud, "Because I co-labor with you. Where you are, I am. You were doing construction. I was there with you doing construction."

We continued to walk and I had many questions which I did not ask out loud. He knew my thoughts and answered my questions.

I looked into His eyes, and they kept changing colors. They were beautiful. Looking into His eyes was like looking into a kaleidoscope, not the unvarying color in what we would consider typical human eye color.

Everything in heaven was bright, not blinding but white, except Jesus in His blue jeans and blue plaid shirt and this perfect grass under our bare feet.

As we walked, I noticed after each step Jesus took, the grass bounced back up like He didn't even step there. When I realized Jesus was not leaving footprints, I turned to see if I was leaving footprints. I wasn't, so again I thought, There are no footprints. I didn't say any of this out loud. But He responded, "Do you know why that is?"

I answered no and He said, "Because nothing will ever be remembered against you in heaven. Not even your footsteps."

We headed toward something like a gate. I knew the gate represented a decision point and going through would mean stepping into another corridor of heaven.

As we walked closer to the corridor, I remembered my family, my grandkids, my wife, and all the loved ones on earth. Heaven was amazing and I wanted to experience all of it but I didn't know about leaving my loved ones. So I asked out loud, "Can I live?"

He wore a big smile on His face when He answered, "Yes."

In that moment, we turned left instead of going straight through the gate. This felt like a point of no return, the pivot between returning to earth or staying in heaven.

Then we saw this multitude of people who didn't have faces.

These are the ones!

I said out loud, "Who are all these people?"

He said, "These are the ones who would not have made heaven if you had chosen to stay here today."

Then I came to in the ambulance. I heard the paramedics talking to the hospital, saying I had a broken arm, broken leg, and a fractured skull. Later my wife Shelly told me when I arrived at the hospital, 21 people were in the waiting room, praying for me.

Three different times, the nurses came to the waiting room with the same report: fractured skull, broken arm, and a broken leg. The third time they added severe brain trauma to the diagnoses.

The fourth update came from the doctor who said, "We're not sure what's going on. When he came in, the x-rays showed a broken arm, broken leg, and a fractured skull. Now we cannot find evidence of those fractures. We checked again and know he still has severe brain trauma."

I was in the hospital for three days. During those three days, my healing was supernaturally quick. Even my stitches scabbed up. They told Shelly I would probably sleep the whole time I was there but I hardly slept. I really wanted to go home.

They said I couldn't go unless I could pass certain physical tests. By the third day, I was up walking around, climbing stairs, and going to the bathroom.

That third day, they said, "We don't know what to do with you now because we can't find anything wrong with you." They had to let me out the third day.

What it means

I'll talk more about what happened in the hospital and additional healing after I got out and I'll share what led up to the accident but let's go back to this event in heaven.

After I asked Jesus if I could live and He said yes, I saw a huge host of people. Jesus said they were the ones who would not have made it to heaven if I had chosen to stay there.

So many people stood in that crowd—the thought was staggering, and still is. I want to do all I can in this life to reach every person I see so they don't lose out on heaven.

If I had not accepted His yes, this is what it would have looked like.

I would not be here on the earth, so Shelly would be a widow. My children and grandchildren would no longer have their dad and grandfather in their lives. My church and ministry wouldn't exist. Many would not have heard of Jesus or been touched by His love through me. You wouldn't be holding this book.

God has a similar desire for your life, for you to take up your yes and be faithful to see people come to Jesus. Isaiah tells us about taking up his yes to God.

"Then I heard the voice of the Lord, saying, 'Whom shall I send, and who will go for Us?' Then I said, 'Here am I. Send me!'" (Isaiah 6:8, NASB1995).

Mary the mother of Jesus also said yes. When the angel told her she had found favor and the Holy Spirit would come upon her, she had a simple answer to this complex announcement.

She said, "Behold, the bondslave of the Lord; may it be done to me according to your word" (Luke 1:38, NASB1995). She said yes and then she carried out that yes with her life. Her yes changed the course of history and touches every human life.

Altering history

Your yes could change human history, too. It can set the stage for another person's yes. Abraham had no idea what was ahead of him when he left Ur but he said yes when God called him to leave that place and go to the place God called him (see Genesis 12). Because of his obedience, the entire nation of Israel came into existence and from that nation, Mary became the mother of Jesus, who would provide eternal life to any who receive it.

Sometimes we are told salvation means we pray a simple prayer and that's the end of it—you have your eternal salvation. You do have salvation but you can have and be and do so much more by living a life centered in Jesus. That's the only way you can fulfill your yes.

Sometimes there is pain in the yes. Sometimes we say yes without knowing how much sacrifice will be involved, even family (see Luke 14:26). But fulfilling your yes is the most satisfying way to live.

What Is Your Yes?

God has a yes for each of us. When Jesus was here on earth, He sent His disciples out with these words: "the harvest is plentiful, but the laborers are few" (Luke 10:2, NASB1995). He wants to trust you with a yes.

Maybe you don't know what being a laborer means. What harvest does He mean? Maybe you see a big gap between your life and mine. You've never been to heaven and you don't see people impacted by love or salvation every day.

If you get centered in Jesus, the trajectory of your life will radically transform. When you co-labor with Jesus, you'll see people changed. In the next chapter we're going to look at what that means. Join me.

2. WHAT YOUR YES MEANS

When I asked Jesus if I could live and He said yes, He was offering me the opportunity to partner or co-labor with Him. Everyone is born with a purpose and a priority from God. "For I know the plans that I have for you, . . . plans for welfare and not for calamity to give you a future and a hope" (Jeremiah 29:11, NASB1995).

When God said yes to me, He trusted me with saying yes to Him and all He has for me during the rest of my time on earth. The best way for me to do that was to live centered up.

Being centered up in Jesus means something. It's how you step into your yes. Living centered up is what you do after you pray for salvation. Failure to learn how to live centered up can keep you from your yes.

Living Centered Up

We will talk about what it means to live centered up throughout the book but for now, let's look at the foundations.

When you first pray to receive Jesus, you become centered up with Him. You're no longer on the outside or somewhere in between, but you are centered with Jesus because you received Him in your heart. That means you are "a new creature; the old things passed away; behold, new things have come" (2 Corinthians 5:17b, NASB1995).

Now, what you do with that is up to you. How you grow is up to you. My advice is to get in the Word of God daily and stay in the Word of God. You also need to be part of a local church. The author of Hebrews reminds us about "not forsaking our own assembling together" (Hebrews 10:25, NASB1995). By attending church in person, you can find a mentor or discipleship program to help you grow in spiritual understanding.

When you do, you begin to understand more and more how to live centered up.

You will stop leaning on your own understanding and lean on the very Word of God. "Trust in the Lord with all your heart and do not lean on your own understanding. In all your ways acknowledge Him, and He will make your paths straight" (Proverbs 3:5,6, NASB1995).

What about problems?

We all have struggles. The wise thing to do when you encounter problems is to pray this way: God, I want to understand what You are doing in my life and understand the solution to the problem I see. I need Your power to receive all You have for me.

God wants to give you a solution to that problem, but He wants you to be in the center of His will. Here's why: when you're in the middle of God's will, no matter what the world throws at you, you can count it joy.

You might not understand the problem and you might not know how to handle it, but you can be filled with joy. Let God do what He does and work through those situations because the God we serve takes joy in making all things work together for good (see Romans 8:28).

You're not always going to understand everything about God, and that's okay. The more you get in the Word of God, the more you're going to understand. The more you center up and tighten up that center when you're with Him, the better off you're going to be because you start understanding things more.

King Solomon, the wisest man who ever lived, tells us "The fear of the Lord is the beginning of knowledge; fools despise wisdom and instruction" (Proverbs 1:7, NASB1995). He also said, "The fear of the Lord is the beginning of wisdom, and the knowledge of the Holy One is understanding" (Proverbs 9:10, NASB1995).

When we look at what Solomon said about the fear of the Lord, we get this: Knowledge of the Holy One is understanding. You will grow in understanding when you grow in the knowledge of God and who He is, especially who He is in you.

Living From The Center

I challenge you to center up with God. The only way you're going to do that is to have a fear of the Lord. There's a difference between the dread and terror of Him, because you don't know Him, and godly fear, which is profound respect and deep reverence for how powerful, majestic, and wonderful He is.

I understand more about the Word of God now than I did years ago. Back then, I was ignorant and didn't know anything compared to what I understand now after years of living centered up. The more you dig in the Word of God, the more you feel like you were ignorant but now you've come to understand something.

It's good to be in the center of God's will because you perceive things differently than people who are not. They cannot understand life correctly. You are no longer leaning on your own understanding but on God Himself and being centered up in Him.

When you center up, watch what He does with that, how He grows you and changes things in your life. Remember, He knows best in every situation.

What centering up does not mean

The term "centered" has been taken up by many communities, the study of psychology, New Age practitioners, yoga teachers and many more. I want to be very clear my referral is to Jesus, not breathing or emptying your mind or any other thing than growing in intimacy with God. To do that you need your own personal study of the Word, time spent with Holy Spirit, and accountability within a body of people who love Jesus. An integral part of this lifestyle is allowing God to refine us of all impurity. We will look at these things in more depth.

When you choose Jesus, He becomes the centerpiece of daily living.

Daily living

As you go through your day learning to understand God and staying centered up with Him, you also have the opportunity to make everything you do count in the Kingdom of God. The Apostle Paul said, "Whatever you do, do your work heartily, as for the Lord rather than for men, knowing that from the Lord you will receive the reward of the inheritance. It is the Lord Christ whom you serve" (Colossians 3:23-24, NASB1995).

Paul's counsel to the Colossians was "simple and straightforward: Just go ahead with what you've been given. You received Christ Jesus, the Master; now live him" (Colossians 2:6-7, MSG). When you "live Jesus," you will co-labor with Him.

Co-Laboring

If you've never heard the term co-laboring, it means to work together with God for His purposes. "For we are co-workers in God's service" (1 Corinthians 3:9, NIV). He initiates the concept by co-laboring with us because He loves us. Eventually, this becomes a two-way street where we learn to co-labor with Him from a place of love and gratitude. We need to understand His ways to get His work done.

Where co-laboring started

"In the beginning God created the heavens and the earth. The earth was without form, and void" (Genesis 1:1-2, KJV). God the Father co-labored with Jesus and the Holy Spirit to create the earth. Jesus, who was The Word, spoke creation into being. The Holy Spirit hovered over the water to bring forth life and the three co-labored together.

God formed the earth for us to have a place to stand. God's co-laboring for our benefit was to build a foundation for us. Then God invited Adam and Eve to co-labor with him. He told them, "Be fruitful and multiply; fill the earth and subdue it; have dominion over the fish of the sea, over the birds of the air, and over every living thing that moves on the earth" (Genesis 1:28, KJV). He wanted us to steward the earth He created.

God had to do the co-laboring first. He started with forming the world, along with its creatures, and creating man. Then man, Adam, labored; he co-labored with the godhead.

When Adam and Eve had children, they brought forth the line which Jesus would come from. We see Jesus in the New Testament co-laboring with the disciples so they could learn to co-labor with Him. Jesus co-labored and made the way. Now we as His disciples need to share the gospel. When we share the gospel, we co-labor with Him and with each other.

Your yes is valuable. We all go through trials and tribulations to see how far we'll carry out our yes. If God can trust you with a little, He'll give you more.

Old Testament examples

God offers you a yes and your yes has a story inside it, just like Joseph's. He was the obnoxious younger brother who was sold into slavery by his own brothers and later served Pharaoh in Egypt. His yes came when he saved multitudes of people by interpreting the dream God gave Pharaoh to store the harvest in preparation for the coming famine. Later, he became the most powerful man in Egypt after Pharaoh. All of this came from his yes to God.

King David's life reveals a good example of co-laboring. David learned relationship with God by worshiping God in the field with the sheep long before he became king. When he visited his brothers and saw Goliath mocking his God, he wanted to confront him. At that moment, God co-labored with David to defeat the giant.

Later in his life, David became a great king but he made mistakes. He needed to co-labor with God to recover from his infidelity with Bathsheba and the attempt to cover his sin.

Many others in the Old Testament co-labored with God. I encourage you to study them.

New Testament examples

You can look at every one of the disciples' stories and see how Jesus went after them before they turned and came after Him. He went to them first. "Hey, come follow me."

Before meeting Jesus, they followed their religion the best they could. They did their duty, co-laboring out of obligation to the godhead. When Jesus called, they turned their religion into true reality by following the true Savior out of a true love. They began to serve God and follow Jesus with their whole hearts. They co-labored with Him, doing what He needed them to do for people to come. Luke 10 shows the disciples co-laboring when He sent them out two by two to express the love they received from Him.

Jesus was on earth fully human, and He co-labored in prayer to God in the Garden of Gethsemane. We see His struggle in Matthew 26, Mark 14, and Luke 22. His prayer was along these lines: "Hey, I don't really want to go to the cross, but because You are who You are, not My will but Your will be done. I'll do it."

The Fruit of Co-Laboring

More fruit is produced from co-laboring with God out of love than from a mindset of duty. Days before the accident where I went to heaven, God gave me a series of three visions. The first one illustrates how co-laboring with Him produces more fruit.

The first vision

In the vision, I stood in heaven with Jesus and I saw a tree full of fruit. I could see all the leaves and branches on the tree along with the fruit. He said, "This is your life." He was showing the fruit in my life from Him co-laboring with me.

Then He showed me another tree so full of fruit, I couldn't see the leaves or branches because it had so much fruit on it. He was showing me the result of co-laboring with Him. He said, "Walk in the fullness."

Then, we walked back to the first tree. He stepped inside of me. When He raised His arms, I raised mine with His and an ax appeared. Together as one, we chopped that tree down. What He had for me was the most important thing, oneness.

The act of chopping the first tree together was an example of Him co-laboring with me. The first tree produced fruit, but it wasn't the most fruit. The second tree showed the result of me co-laboring with Him which yielded a tree full of fruit.

The fruit on the second tree when I co-labored with Him was the multitude who would not have made heaven if I had chosen to remain in heaven instead of returning to earth to co-labor with Him. God immediately sent another vision.

The second vision

God showed me a whirlwind which began to spin. Holy Spirit said, "This is your new name. Your name is Whirlwind." He began squeezing from the top down into a pencil-thin whirlwind. He said, "I'm squeezing everything out of you that's not of Me."

When olive oil is harvested, it requires the olives to be squeezed.

Then he opened the whirlwind from the top so it looked like a funnel. He said, "Now, I'm giving you full access to bring heaven down to earth."

He's still in that squeezing process. He opens the top and lets heaven come down, putting fresh oil out of me into the world. The more I bring heaven down in my life, the more it pushes oil out at the bottom of this whirlwind.

The first vision was with Jesus, the second was with Holy Spirit, and then a third vision with the Father.

The third vision

Suddenly, I was with the Father. He was behind me and I could hear His audible voice. We were walking in the peaks of the mountains, hovering or walking in midair over top of the different valleys. He stopped at a valley and said, "I always want you to live on high. Do you see the people down in the valley?"

I said, "Yes."

He said, "Will you minister to them?"

I answered yes. I didn't realize I was saying yes to Martinsville.

When I saw Jesus in heaven wearing blue jeans and a blue plaid shirt, He said He was co-laboring with me. I was doing construction the day of the accident so He was co-laboring with me as He did in Jacob's life.

Jacob wanted the blessing (see Genesis 27) but God wanted Jacob. Like Jacob, God came to me and co-labored with me until I came to co-labor with Him.

A new vision

During the pandemic when public buildings and churches were closing, the Lord told me to keep moving, not to stop. People lined up in their cars and we went out to pray for them. In that season, I started building out the interior of our last church building and God gave me another vision.

I saw heaven again, the same place we were after the wreck, but this time there were sheep in the grass. Everything was still bright, with the beautiful grass and sheep grazing, but Jesus and I each wore a white robe instead of jeans.

He said, "Now you're co-laboring with Me." First He co-labored with me to get me, because He saw the value in me. Then I co-labored with Him and this is what people see—me co-laboring with Him.

Please understand I can do nothing without God. My ability to co-labor is based on four foundational pillars Jesus taught me: Love, Identity, Freedom, and Encounter. These four words make the acronym LIFE.

This foundation and the four pillars form the structure for my yes.

3. THE FOUNDATION OF CO-LABORING

It's easy to ask whether I was co-laboring with God when I had the wreck that killed me. I started the day right by co-laboring but later rolled into disobedience. I went to work at a house in Martinsville right after we got back from Bethel in Redding, CA.

God co-labored with me by warning me around 3 pm to leave the work site. I heard the Lord say, "Leave the job now." I told the guys to pack up because we were leaving early.

Then, someone important to me asked me to stay to meet up. I said, "No, I'm leaving now." This conversation happened several times and I was held up by at least half an hour. I didn't obey and got into a life-changing mess.

When you co-labor with God, you're going to make better decisions because you're doing it with His perspective. Instead of leaning on your own way of thinking, you lean on every word of God to make those right decisions.

This is what God showed me in the first vision of chopping down the old tree where He had to co-labor with me before I could produce more fruit by co-laboring with Him. Possibly, if I had not died in the accident, I would not be co-laboring with Him but doing what I want.

That death was a transitioning to a new level where the things I wanted in my old life didn't matter compared to doing what God wants me to do. You may not die physically in a wreck but dying to self by putting God's desires above your own is central to co-laboring. When we co-labor with Him, it produces everything He wants for us and those affected by our yes to Him.

God wasn't mad at me for failing to obey when he told me to leave the worksite. He loved me in spite of my disobedience, just as He loves you. He forgave me for disobedience and He forgives you. That love and forgiveness makes all the difference. It helps you learn to walk in obedience.

Learning Obedience

Shelly and I learned more about obedience after the wreck. I had a lot of healing to do after coming home from the hospital. We were established in Indiana but loved the beach. After several months of healing, we drove our RV back to Destin, Florida, where we parked a couple of blocks off the beach within easy walking distance.

We began renovation work and during that time we were offered a full-time ministry job in Destin. We decided to move there.

As we prepared to move, we planned to tell our sons, "Hey, we're going to move to Destin. I hope you guys come and bring all the grandkids." We came back to Indiana to get ready for the move and God said, "You're not going to Destin."

I said, "What do you mean?"

He said, "I need you to go to Martinsville."

I said, "I am not going to Martinsville. No, I'm going to Destin."

He said, "No, I need..."

Three days in a row He spoke to me. Each day was the same discussion. On the third, He told me, "You said you would."

I said, "When did I say I would?"

He reminded me of the visions in the last chapter when I said yes, and I said, "All right, I'll go. But You've got to talk to my wife about it because she's always wanted to be in Destin."

A happy wife is a happy life. She said yes.

Our current ministry is a result of that yes. We rode the wave of obedience from Florida to Martinsville. During that season, we received many prophetic words around Martinsville and being in ministry and they've all come about in various ways. We didn't know it would be a church and full-time ministry, later expanding into the healing waters of baptism.

Early in the ministry, the Lord dropped these four words into my spirit as pillars of our ministry.

Love. Identity. Freedom. Encounter.

You can see the first letters of each word form the word "life." Each pillar is integrated into the others. These pillars are based on the foundation of Jesus where we learn to live the centered-up life.

Why we need a foundation

God designed us to function best within structure. We all need rules to follow. An essential part of structure is foundation. Your foundation has to be right.

Foundation is a big part of a healthy Christian walk. We see this in the natural, when considering construction. In Indiana, building codes call for digging

32-36 inches below ground to pour a footer because the freeze line is there. If you are above the freeze line, your foundation will crack. If you dig below the freeze line, the foundation won't crack because the earth doesn't change there. The cold doesn't get that deep so it doesn't break the foundation. The foundation has to be right; it has to be dug deep enough.

Jesus made a foundation for you and me to enter into the kingdom of God when He paid the price on Calvary. His death bought our eternal salvation.

What forms your foundation

I see some who profess salvation but have no fruit. I see people who say they love God but they walk around with a façade, looking like the world and don't have the foundation of Jesus Christ.

They are based in the world, because God created the world and we are here all walking together. But they have no solid foundation to stand on with Christ. They build their lives on a weak, manmade foundation, like a job or money.

The Apostle Paul talks to this kind of people in the church of Corinth.

> "And I, brethren, could not speak to you as to spiritual men, but as to men of flesh, as

to infants in Christ. I gave you milk to drink, not solid food; for you were not yet able to receive it. Indeed, even now you are not yet able" (1 Corinthians 3:1-2, NASB1995).

Why does Paul say he cannot speak to them as spiritual men? They were still doing their own thing, living their lives the way they wanted to live. He calls them men of flesh, still living in the flesh as infants in Christ.

We all live in this body or temple God created, but living in the flesh is living as a baby. Paul tells them he has to feed them milk and not solid food because they are not able yet to receive solid food (1 Corinthians 3:2).

The flesh is what we don't want to live from. Our goal is to live according to the kingdom principle of living from the Spirit and, by doing that, bringing heaven to earth. While it's true we live in a physical body, we should not be living from the flesh. If you're a true Christian, you should be seeking to live from the Spirit.

This is serious business. We're talking a kingdom principle. We're talking souls.

What do we have to do to get to the place to receive solid food? We're going to have to grow up and put away childish things, which often lead to sin.

Sin in the church

The church, in general, has become nominal, meaning many people in the church are going to heaven but that's the extent of their spiritual lives. They haven't learned to put away sin and end up getting wounded by it.

When someone within a specific church body sins because they live in the flesh, a tourniquet gets put on the wound without addressing the root issue. Then the church becomes lame and hurting. We must repair these long-lost things in the church.

We want to bring heaven to earth and live from heaven. What we do on earth to get other people into heaven is not to tear someone down but to build them up.

They might have problems and so do you. That's why in John chapter 8 when the accusers wanted to know what Jesus would do about the woman caught in adultery, He wrote on the ground. We don't know what He wrote, but He wrote, and then all the accusers walked away.

The best way to build others up is to build upon the foundation of Christ.

Be careful how you build

> For we are God's fellow workers; you are God's field, God's building. According to the grace of God which was given to me, like a wise master builder I laid a foundation, and another is building on it. But each man must be careful how he builds on it. For no man can lay a foundation other than the one which is laid, which is Jesus Christ (1 Corinthians 3:9-11a, NASB1995).

Our foundation is laid upon the foundation of Christ. If you're laying your foundation on something other than Christ, you need to ask Holy Spirit to show you how to shift things.

"Now if any man builds on the foundation with gold, silver, precious stones, wood, hay, straw, each man's work will become evident; for . . . it is to be revealed with fire, and the fire itself will test the quality of each man's work" (1 Corinthians 3:11b-13, NASB1995).

If someone built their life on money or other worthless things, their foundation will be tried by the fire when they get to heaven. The worthless things will be burned.

"If any man's work which he has built on it remains, he will receive a reward. If any man's work is burned up, he will suffer loss; but he himself will be saved, yet so as through fire" (1 Corinthians 3:14-15, NASB1995).

If you build your life on things that burn up, the Bible says when you get to heaven you will suffer loss, but you will be saved. Instead of building your foundation on money, are you taking the money God gave you and building on the foundation God has brought into your region?

What Comes After the Foundation

Paul told them " . . . I laid a foundation, and another is building on it. But each man must be careful how he builds on it. For no man can lay a foundation other than . . . Jesus Christ (1 Corinthians 3:10-11, NASB1995).

If you look at this from a construction viewpoint, with our foundation of Jesus, the next thing we need is the pillars and they are love, identity, freedom and encounter. A brief description of the four pillars follows next.

4. FOUR PILLARS

I am building upon a foundation, and Christ is the
foundation I'm building on. Now we need the pillars that
go on the foundation. Here you'll find an overview of
four pillars essential to building a life centered on Jesus.
We'll take a deeper look into each pillar in later
chapters.

First Pillar: Love

His greatest gift to you is to love you. Slowly read aloud
the following words from Ephesians.

> Watch what God does, and then you do it,
> like children who learn proper behavior
> from their parents. Mostly what God does
> is love you. Keep company with him and
> learn a life of love. Observe how Christ
> loved us. His love was not cautious but
> extravagant. He didn't love in order to get
> something from us but to give everything of

himself to us. Love like that (Ephesians 5:1-2, MSG).

From the Bible

"Though I speak with the tongues of men and of angels, but have not love, I have become sounding brass or a clanging cymbal" (1 Corinthians 13:1, NKJV). These verses tell us whatever we do "profits me nothing" if it lacks love.

The chapter goes on to tell us what love does. "Love suffers long . . . love does not envy; love does not parade itself, is not puffed up; does not behave rudely . . ." (1 Corinthians 13:4-5, NKJ).

At the end of the chapter, Paul tells us "And now abide faith, hope, love, these three; but the greatest of these is love" (1 Corinthians 13:13, NKJV). The Greek word for this love is *agape*, the unconditional love of God who chose to love us all the way to the cross.

Second Pillar: Identity

When you ask Jesus Christ to come into your life and live in your heart, forgive you of your sins, and cleanse you from all unrighteousness, He brings life to you. He offers you new life and you become His.

In that new life, you are accepted. You are forgiven. You are chosen. You are free. You are a new person. You are part of God's family, a true son or daughter, and now heir of the kingdom of God.

It's important for you to know identity is not something you *achieve*, but something you *receive* through the living Word of God. It's also important to realize we have sin habits to overcome. Paul tells us to "work out our salvation with fear and trembling" (Philippians 2:12, NASB1995).

The following verses from the Bible reveal parts of our identity.

Finding identity in the Bible

God dreamed of and thought of us before He created the world. "He chose us in Him before the foundation of the world, that we would be holy and blameless before Him in love" (Ephesians 1:4, NASB1995).

We were created in the image of God. "So God created man in His own image, in the image of God He created him; male and female He created them" (Genesis 1:27, NASB1995). I'm grateful I'm created in the image of God.

If you know Jesus, you can step into the inheritance God has for you. We are heirs and have an inheritance in God. ". . . did God not choose the poor of this world to be rich in faith and heirs of the kingdom which He promised to those who love Him?" (James 2:5, NASB1995).

You are protected by God and God is with you. "For the Lord . . . does not abandon His godly ones; They are protected forever" (Psalm 37:28, NASB1995).

You are precious to him. You are part of something very important. ". . . you are precious in My sight . . . you are honored and I love you" (Isaiah 43:4, NASB1995).

God gives you strength. "The God of Israel Himself gives strength and power to the people" (Psalm 68:35, NASB1995).

He listens to you and you are blessed. "For God listens to the poor" (Psalm 69:33, MSG).

Jesus went away so Holy Spirit could come and live in you. "These things I have spoken to you while remaining with you. But the Helper, the Holy Spirit whom the Father will send in My name, He will teach you all things, and remind you of all that I said to you" (John 14:25-26, NASB1995).

Because you are rescued, you're now a citizen of heaven. ". . . you are no longer strangers and foreigners, but you are fellow citizens with the saints, and are of God's household" (Ephesians 2:19, NASB1995).

Living your identity

Many people in the world today and in Bible times struggled with identity. God's Word is the only way to find who you are, to discover the identity God has given you, and to receive from Him. You must believe this is the living Word of God. You must believe all of the Word of God to be true because it is true.

We must understand the fullness of the Word to be able to understand who we are in Christ. No anonymous program will find your identity for you. Most programs will lock you into the old you, which was a lie from the beginning.

Your identity in Him is who you are. It's not what you've done or any kind of a lifestyle you live. Who you are is what the Word says you are.

Speak identity from God's Word into your life, not the negative things or the lies. When you stand in the mirror, you say, "I am God's amazing son or daughter, and He loves me. He cherishes me. I'm valuable. I am worth it because He says so."

Choose your source

You have two options. You can either find your identity from what the world says or you can find your identity from what God says. "How long will you hesitate between two opinions? If the Lord is God, follow Him" (1 Kings 18:21, NASB1995).

Ask yourself how long you will hesitate between the two identities, from the world or from the Father. Those who follow the world's identity receive it from a false god and they walk in that identity. We must walk in the identity God has given us. You have a choice who speaks identity into you: the world or God.

We cannot let our identity lie in things like jobs or possessions or people we know, but we must let it lie in Jesus and Him alone, because He's the one who will never fail us.

When you walk in who you are, you won't be ashamed of who you were. You won't be afraid to ask God for the things you need from Him.

When you live in alignment with the true word of God, your thoughts and behavior match your priorities, values, and beliefs. There's no longer a need to chase after the things of the world.

Your character is going to come out and you will walk intentionally for Him with the ability to live by your deepest values through the identity God gave you.

Third Pillar: Freedom

The moment we surrender our lives to Jesus is the moment we receive our identity and the moment we have complete freedom in Christ. We're free of the past and the sins we committed in the past, but freedom comes at a cost. If you think otherwise, read the Bible. Read what Jesus went through, what He paid to set us free of all things.

When Jesus paid the ultimate price for you and me on Calvary to have freedom, in that moment we became a new creature. "Therefore if any man be in Christ, he is a new creature: old things are passed away; behold, all things are become new" (2 Corinthians 5:17, KJV).

If you're bound to the past or sins of the past, you need to discover how God sees you by studying the Word and being in community with believers. As you go further in getting to know God, you get baptized, you remain accountable in the Body, you die to sin and you come out a new creature in a new lifestyle, living new things new ways.

"Call upon Me in the day of trouble; I will deliver you, and you shall glorify Me" (Psalms 50:15, NKJV). God tells us we will glorify Him when we call out in days of trouble because He wants to deliver us. His heart is to deliver us and see us free from the bondage of sin.

He has plans to give you the future you hope for (see Jeremiah 29:11).

Just because we have salvation doesn't mean we walk totally 100% free. All of us struggle with something. We all have battles, things to overcome, whether it's in our own lives, with our children, friends and loved ones, or in our jobs, or something else. We want freedom for them or for our own lives.

God wants you to know complete freedom. Jesus didn't pay the price just for you to be free from your past sins. He went all the way to the cross to pay for all of your sins, even in the future. When you fall into temptation to sin, Jesus said He's an advocate for that sin. " . . . if anyone sins, we have an Advocate with the Father, Jesus Christ the righteous" (1 John 2:1, NASB1995).

You confess that sin. "If we confess our sins, he is faithful and just to forgive us our sins, and to cleanse us from all unrighteousness" (1 John 1:9, KJV).

It doesn't mean we continue in sin so grace abounds (see Romans 6:1-6). It means we continue to walk in the fullness of God. We don't choose sin; we step away from sin. But if we do sin, Jesus is there to forgive us because He already paid the price for past, present, and future sins.

Fourth Pillar: Encounter

We just discussed what it means to be free from all the things holding us back from the fullness of God and what He has for us. One thing He has for us is encounters with Him to develop us in healing, hearing, and fulfilling our yes.

Jesus' encounters

Jesus demonstrated many encounters, including time travel from point A to point B in an instant. Here are some examples.

When Jesus began his public ministry, He read from Isaiah 61 in the synagogue. He told them, "Today this Scripture has been fulfilled in your hearing" (see Luke 4:21) and the people were filled with rage.

This is how they responded: ". . . they got up and drove Him out of the city, and brought Him to the crest of the hill on which their city had been built, so they could throw Him down from the cliff. But He passed through their midst and went on His way" Luke 4:29-30, NASB1995). He disappeared from the cliff top in a moment.

A similar story is told at the end of John 8 when the Jews wanted to stone Jesus for saying, "Truly, truly I say to you, before Abraham was born, I am." (John 8:58, NASB1995). He disappeared and they didn't know where He went.

Jesus was fully man as well as fully God. He operated on this earth as man. When He had the encounters, He had them as a man. When He said to the wind, "Peace be still" (Mark 4:39, KJV), He was a human speaking to the wind.

Jesus had an encounter with the devil when He was tested in the desert (see Luke 4). What would Jesus do? He knew the Word of God and spoke it so the enemy had to flee.

Matthew 8, Mark 5, and Luke 8 tell the story of Jesus meeting a man troubled by demons. When He encountered the head demon in the man, Jesus told all the demons to leave the man and they went into the swine. We can see how the encounters Jesus had changed things around Him because the man ministered to his whole city.

If you want encounters, go and hide in the secret place. Hunger and thirst for Him. If you lack in that, tell the Lord you want more of Him, and He will meet you. You can daily encounter Jesus. When you do, you begin to build your life on His foundation.

The first pillar you need is God's great love for you. How well do you know His love?

5. FIRST PILLAR: LOVE

Let's look a little closer at God's greatest gift to you.
When Jesus walked to the cross, He walked all the way
in love. He saw what the people were doing and how
they were.

They hollered, "Crucify Him." Not just once but
many times. His mom was crying and many were
shocked. Others just wanted Him dead. Jesus knew the
price He had to pay.

Yet He walked all the way to the cross in love and
with love. What an amazing God and Savior we serve.
Not only did He walk to the cross with love, He laid
down His life in power. While on the cross, His arms
were spread in compassion. Before He took His last
breath, He said, "Father, forgive them, for they don't
know what they're doing" (Luke 23:24, NASB1995).

His love was extravagant. He didn't love in order to
get something from us, but to give everything of Himself
to us. That's how we're supposed to love one another.

We're here to help each other by giving of ourselves as He did.

God's Design Is the Best Design

Matthew 22:37 tells us, "Thou shalt love the Lord thy God with all thy heart, and with all thy soul, and with all thy mind"(KJV). Jesus tells the people this is the first commandment and there is a second one like it.

We must learn the first commandment first. If you don't love God with all your heart, with all your soul, with all your mind, you won't be able to fulfill the second commandment. We must have a love relationship with God. He makes the first move by loving us and then gives us the power to respond in love to Him.

Jesus said, "Thou shalt love thy neighbor as thyself." Before you can love your neighbor, you have to love yourself by the power of God's love. I've ministered to thousands of people and most of the people I come in contact with don't know how to love themselves. God gives us that power, but often, the inability to love ourselves is tied to not forgiving ourselves.

If you are a Christian, if you know Jesus paid the ultimate price and forgave you, then you have walked in the first commandment of loving God with all your heart, mind, and soul. If that is where you are living, all the bad things you've done are gone because Jesus forgave them.

Now in His forgiveness, you can forgive yourself. Once you've forgiven yourself, going out and loving others is part of who you are. When God is our center, we have His ability to love others and draw them to the love of our Father.

Think of it like the gravitational pull of the sun keeping our earth on track. We are drawn to the Son of God (sun) and His powerful love (gravitational pull) keeps us on track spreading the Kingdom by loving others.

Learning to live like this is not a lifestyle where you are in the center and you pull Him in because He was on the outside. In that situation, when something breaks down, you realize you need God so you ask, "Can You come here and be the center for a minute?"

When you live with God at the center, you see a situation on the outside, and you pray, "God, can You go out here and help me with this situation? Because I want to stay right here close to You. I want to stay in the light because You are the light. I don't want to be in the shadows anymore, God. I like being close to You because there's no darkness around You."

Knowing God's voice

When we love someone and spend time with them, we know their voice. It's one of the ways we know we are in relationship. Genesis 3 reveals that Adam and Eve learned to recognize God's voice because God was present with them daily. They walked in the presence of God until the moment they made the wrong choice. When the enemy came, they listened to him. He seemed reasonable but he always deceives and can speak things that seem good.

We need to recognize which voice is the enemy and which is the voice of God. As you practice recognizing the voice of God, you come to know that you know that you know it's God. This way, when the enemy comes to speak, you can automatically put him behind and recognize: Nope, that's not God. That's not His voice, and that's not His character.

God encounters each person in the way that best fits them. These encounters can be public or private, loud or subtle, but they will speak to you in the way God knows is personal to you. Whatever your encounter looks like, you are learning to recognize God's voice.

Learning to discern God's voice

There are several ways I hear God's voice. Sometimes I hear it audibly, sometimes internally, sometimes I get a gut feeling. It can also be an image, as real as seeing Jesus sitting beside me in the car.

When I need to know where a voice is coming from, I consider three sources: God, myself, or the enemy. I've practiced it so much I know the difference, whether it's God, the enemy, or if it's me. I know when I get out of that center place because the result always brings havoc.

I've tested whose voice am I hearing and kept a record of that testing. When I tested, I would hear a certain thing and follow through with what I heard. I would clearly see when the outcome wasn't from God. Then I would know the voice I heard wasn't God's.

The enemy comes to steal, kill, and destroy. His goal is to break you financially and spiritually and mentally. So I test to see if this is the voice of the enemy. Is this something that could break me? Is it persistent? Is it something that's rushing me? Is this a case of my feelings looking at the situation instead of Jesus?

If it's not God, I don't want to be a part of it.

Individual hearing

Anyone who is close to God can discern His voice. Recognizing God's voice starts with studying the Word of God and prayer. It also requires being still to listen. When you do that, God's going to develop your ability to recognize His voice in the way that is specific to you. How federal agents know money is counterfeit is by studying the real thing, not studying endless counterfeit bills. We must do the same.

The enemy works hard to fool us, so people who don't spend time in God's Word can be blind to the influence of the enemy in our culture for harm. When we study and know the real thing, we recognize the counterfeit voice immediately because we know it's not in God's character.

Of course each person has to hear God in their specific way. Many hear the still, small voice of God internally. Not everyone will hear the audible voice of God. Not everyone will have images or visions. Not everyone has dreams of Jesus coming to them as some Muslims report, Muslims who are hungry for truth since it's difficult for them to access outside teaching.

Even a new believer can hear his voice. The one who just stepped into relationship with God heard God somewhere. Now they must determine how they heard Him, whether it's through a preacher or some other way. They can start with that small step and think, where did I hear that? How did it come to me? Was it through the audible voice of the pastor? Was it through my heart being tugged in a time of stillness? What was it that made me want to get saved? Once you determine that first key, it is a domino effect from there.

At times, God's voice will tell me in a clear, unpressured, almost commanding voice to do a specific thing. The enemy sounds more like, "Do it now, do it now, do it now, do it now." In those moments, we act out of something besides relationship with God. The important thing is to spend time learning how God is speaking to you every moment of every day.

Daily living

For example, when I'm driving, I can choose four or five different ways to a certain location. I ask the Lord, "Hey, which way are we going today?" Generally, He'll take me one way, and I may find out later there was a roadblock or something going on the other way.

Sometimes the Lord drops things in my spirit or my mind. Then I study it, looking in the Word or searching online to see if the thing I heard resonates with God's ways or if it's some other voice. The other day the thought of coffee dropped in my spirit and I looked it up. If this study had said you should not drink coffee, then I would have thanked God for letting me know.

I make a practice of generosity but I also listen for God's voice. Generally, when God is speaking and I give money to someone, there's a follow-up confirmation. For instance, afterwards when I give, they may say something like, "You don't know how I needed this or how much I've been praying about this." That would be confirmation to me. If I give money out of myself, I just give it, I feel good about it, and that's the end of it. I get no confirmation.

Hearing for Yourself

Because people have to learn to recognize God's voice for themselves, the way they recognize God's voice may be different than the way I recognize it. People will hear Him in their own way. If someone is driving down the road, and a name suddenly drops in their mind, that's the time to ask God what to do with that name.

The other day in my spirit I heard the name of an old high school friend. Billy Boyd (not his real name) just stayed with me and I felt like I was supposed to call him. I asked the Lord what He wanted me to do with this name. I kept getting the impression to call him but I had no way to get hold of him since the last time I was in touch was over 15 years ago.

I called someone to see if they had contact info. It took some time but when I got the number later that day, I called him. I asked if I was talking with Billy Boyd.

He said yes and I identified myself. He said, "Jason? Man, I haven't heard from you in 15-20 years."

I said, "Yeah. Listen man, I'm a Christian now. I felt like the Lord told me to call you."

He said, "I'm sitting here on my floor because I literally have no furniture. My wife just walked out the door with everything in the house. The only thing I have is the landline phone. God told you to call me?"

"Yes, I felt like God told me to call you."

He responded, "That's crazy. Like, really? God said to call me?" He was very moved to hear God cared so much about him that He put Billy on my heart to call after all these years. I got to share God's love with him and pray for him, sowing a seed into his life. By his response of gratitude for my call, I received confirmation the voice I heard was God.

I constantly check in with God all day long, not as a religious obligation, but to stay centered with Him so I am ready to fulfill my yes on an ongoing basis.

Results of obeying God's voice

In 1990 I was in an accident when my first son was still an infant. Our norm in that season was to ride with my son in his pumpkin seat up front while my sister-in-law rode in the back. As we headed home from town that evening, a driver coming from the opposite direction fell asleep at the wheel and crossed the center line. We both were traveling at speed on this highway. My evasive maneuver didn't completely avoid him and he slammed into the front passenger corner of our car, in this 120-mph collision.

Earlier that day, I had listened to God and left my son with a babysitter I normally would not allow to take care of him. If he'd been with me, he would not be here on earth now. My sister-in-law normally would have been with us but that day she went to a different place. The jack in the trunk came through her seat exactly where she always sat. The other passenger was severely injured but alive. I was beyond grateful I obeyed and did not bring my son and sister-in-law with us. By the mercy of God, I had no broken bones.

How does discerning God's voice play out in my yes to God?

If we don't know His voice from the enemy's voice, we're going to get ourselves in trouble by following the wrong thing. It could be the wrong person, the wrong word, the wrong prophecy, the wrong anything. What we follow will change the direction of our whole life, for good or bad.

I've seen people operate in giftings that are not their calling. They love God and aren't willfully being disobedient, but they didn't discern His calling so the Spirit doesn't fall on what they're doing. As a result, other people don't have the encounter with God that was designed for that moment.

Some Christians linger in the shadows instead of saying yes to being in that center place with Jesus. When they linger, they make it to heaven, but they're not going to arrive with the fullest quiver they can have.

What are you doing to show love?

Jesus set the standard by loving people around Him in a way that changed them. This spread from person to person and changed the region, then the rest of the world. Do we live our lives like He did?

Practical ways to love others

Loving people looks like something. Here are some ways we can love others.

- **Be compassionate to others.** Choose compassion toward people around you.

- **Listen to what others say.** Pay close attention to what they're saying. Don't try to trump their story. Just shut up, let them talk, then bless them and walk away.

- **Share a meal.** Invite someone over to your house. People love to go to other people's houses and learn a little more about them.

- **When you eat out, tip 100%.** Let them know Jesus loves them and they're amazing. They'll get the message behind it.

- **Be peaceful to people.** Forgive and let go of grudges. Quit being angry at people. Have a smile on your face.

- **Share the gospel everywhere you go.** You don't have to invite people to church. Just ask people if they know Jesus Christ as their Lord and Savior.

- **Stay in the will of God.** In the midst of ministering to others, stay in love with God, stay in your calling, and stay in your lane.

- **Take the blame for your mistakes.** Learn from them. Be as lenient to others as you are to yourself.

- **Don't hesitate to love,** and don't hesitate to ask somebody for love.

Bottom Line

The summary is this: take His Word to heart. Study it. Know it inside and out. Because in knowing the Word, you're going to know God and you're going to know true love. You will know His voice. You'll know the value of who He is and who you are in Him, in that place He created in His heart for you to rest.

"We love him, because he first loved us" (1 John 4:19, KJV).

Love and My Mother

My mom was an amazing woman; however, she did not grow up in the church. She was married four times by the time I was 16 years old, seeking love in all the wrong places. Some people can't imagine what it would be like to have four dads by the time you're 16 and some can't understand where I was.

Mom sent us to church, but we never were involved in the church, nor was she. She sent us to VBS and stuff just to get us out of her hair. But God was never part of our home life.

I think it's amazing how much she loved us since she could only love us out of the love she knew, the little she had. She whipped us when she disciplined us. There were times we drew away from her because of the discipline, which was more about punishment than discipline. The love of God is so much different because God's discipline is never punishment. It has a purpose of drawing us close to Him.

There are times when people draw away from God because of their own woundedness, not because of the way He loved them. They perceived that disciplined love as punishment instead of discipline and their woundedness draws them away. When you don't know the love of Jesus, you won't know what true love looks like. When you are loved by Jesus or shown love by Jesus, it draws you close to Him.

My mom loved me as she was taught to love. However, I believe she loved me with greater love than she ever received. Somehow, she grabbed hold of that.

Maybe it's because she was looking for love and knew what she wanted.

Untainted love

Mom's love often was a tainted version of what love should look like. When you're loved out of a tainted version of love, you often pull away from the one trying to show you that love. When you are loved by Jesus and you receive it through a wounded heart, you can reject Him and reject that perfect love because of your woundedness.

This is why knowing Jesus and being in the center of His will is so key. When you get disciplined by Him, you appreciate it because you know He's doing it to make your life better and not worse. Experiencing God's love, pure and untainted love, makes all the difference in how you view love toward one another and staying centered in Him.

Love and My Father

When I was two months old, my father left my mother. Over the years I saw him at times but we never had a relationship. Then, one day I had a conversation with him and we came to know each other in a whole different way. We finally understood the other.

Both of us had run away from relationship for so many years, but this time, like the prodigal son parable, we ran toward each other. We were reunited like a father and son should be. In that moment, every wall came down and it was like we had never been apart.

I had just started Life of Love Ministry Center and shared with my dad my yes and all the wonderful things God was doing in my life. I told him of the car crash and my experience with Jesus and all the healings. My dad believed in me for the first time.

I knew now he loved me. He explained that when he left my mom, he had a lot of his own problems and somehow time got away from him. The enemy came in to kill, steal, and destroy our relationship.

While we were talking, he let me pray for him. The pain left his back and he said, "I won't be around long," knowing that he was going to heaven.

The way out

The last words he said to me were so important.

He said, "Son, remember, there's always a way out before the fall."

Truly he was right, for I had a way out before the car crash. And as I look back in my life, I see every time

I sinned or did wrong, God always made a way for me to get out of it before I stepped into anything wrong.

When we finished talking, my father called all of his friends and told them how excited he was that he got his son back. He shared the conversation and the healing with his wife.

I went home to share with my wife the wonderful news that my father and I had reconciled every wound of the past. Until that moment I had never known what it was like to have a true earthly father.

One month later, he was gone.

I left the gym early one morning and almost tripped over a diamond on the ground. I stepped back to pick it up and put it in my pocket. I pondered it all that day, asking the Lord what it meant. The next night I was getting ready to preach and I got the call that my father had passed away. I was partly in shock but I went ahead and preached. Afterward, I told the people to go home and that I would clean up and put the chairs away. When I swept the floor that night, I found a small diamond.

I asked the Lord what it meant, the large diamond the day before and the small diamond I just found. He said, "The big diamond represents your father and the little diamond represents you. You are a chip off of your father. The more you get to know who you are, the more you know who your father was."

I'm getting to know my father through knowing my identity in Christ. This may or may not make sense to you and you may never find a diamond but I want to encourage you. When you find your identity in Christ, you will learn what it means to walk in identity, which is our next pillar.

6. SECOND PILLAR: IDENTITY

Remember our list in the last chapter of ways love could look? We've all experienced times when humans made bad choices that were not from love and hurt us.

When we know our identity, we learn to do life with fewer hurtful choices.

God as Our Main Source

Drastic things happen in all of our lives. If God is not the center of your life so you're grounded in Him, these drastic things can cause you to step away from God. He must be the center and we must be in the center with Him.

Another way to think of identity is to consider God our main source. When Jesus is the center of your life, when you've focused on Him and He is number one in your life, everything else will come into play. He's designed it this way. When the center is right, the outcome is amazing.

Who is your center?

This is the God I want us to align with.

> For He rescued us from the domain of darkness, and transferred us to the kingdom of His beloved Son, in whom we have redemption, the forgiveness of sins. He is the image of the invisible God, the firstborn of all creation: for by Him all things were created, both in the heavens and on earth, visible and invisible, whether thrones, or dominions, or rulers, or authorities—all things have been created through Him and for Him. He is before all things, and in Him all things hold together (Colossians 1:13-17, NASB1995).

This is my main source. Who would not want to serve a God like this? Who would not want this to be your main root to pull from, the source of fulfillment? Being centered is about being grounded in the right source, Christ alone.

Sometimes we put other things at the center of our lives instead of God. When we do, we have put God on the outside circle. When you only pull in God in time of need, He's just a side thing. You have something or someone else in the center place instead of making Jesus the main source of your walk.

Main source or side source

We need to know who we're grounded in to say yes to the right thing. Sometimes we say yes to the enemy, thinking he is the right source. It's easy to say yes to our spouses or children or employers and make them our main source.

They can be a side source, just like a tree has side roots. God lets us have these side feeders. Some trees grow a spread of roots as big as the tree itself and some trees have taproots.

God is like a taproot but often you have other roots in your life. These things shouldn't be your main source but they are part of life. If the source gets cut off, the tree shouldn't die because it still has the tap root; losing your source shouldn't kill you or keep you from functioning.

Jesus will always be there for you, even when others are not. You must say yes to the right source. It's a big deal.

We need Jesus to be that main center, the tap root in our life. All the other things are side feeder roots, the people we bring in our inner circle. Jesus has to be the main source within that inner circle if we are to fulfill our calling.

What do you say yes to

Knowing who we are grounded in means we can say yes to the right thing.

When I visited heaven, God first gave me His yes. Then, I had to choose what to say yes to. I said yes to the right source. We all need to know where we are centered so we say yes to the right thing.

When our yes is in the center place with Jesus, we live out our identity in Him. When we know we are in God and He is in us, we can reach more people and have the full potential to touch all those we're called to reach. We do not miss one thing or person in our life or even one transaction because we know what God needs us to do. We look to God for our calling, not the world.

How the World Views Identity

Each calling is equal to any other calling in God's eyes because God is not a respecter of persons (see Romans 2:8, KJV). The world sees some callings as big or small, but if no sin is greater, then no role is greater.

Each calling has different detail or visibility, but one is not greater than another.

The world can only take you so far in fulfilling your calling. It cannot take you where God wants to take you. You cannot see the things God wants you to see if you think the way the world thinks.

God has a calling for all of us. Humans sometimes see certain callings as greater than others. The truth is all callings are equal, whether pastor, evangelist, mother, encourager, or CEO.

Wrong perspectives

No one is greater or lesser because of their calling, especially if that calling involves a job the world sees as "less than." That is a worldly perspective. Your part might not be as visible as other parts. You still have to be solid in Christ. You still have to grow and live your life according to God, who honors all of us.

It doesn't matter if your job is a trashman. If you're the best trashman there is, you will touch lives for the good. Sometimes people think they have to do something other than their calling. Your life is one piece of the big puzzle, which is the Kingdom of God. Take what God has for you as your piece of the puzzle.

We need all the puzzle pieces

If we don't have the behind-the-scenes people, everything will fall apart. The trashman who takes away the garbage is greater because we have a healthier neighborhood. The person who cleans the bathroom is greater because I get to go to a clean toilet. Grab hold of your value and God's calling for you instead of looking at a job in worldly terms.

The visible one, such as the one who preaches or baptizes or leads worship, is another piece of the puzzle. Learn to see them as puzzle pieces. Those people are no greater than you. Colossians 3:23 tells us, "Whatever you do, do your work heartily, as for the Lord and not for people" (NASB1995).

Wrong sources

If you find your identity lies in your boss or spouse or kids, they've become your source. Maybe you're living your dream through your kids. "I never got to race motorcycles, so I'm gonna make sure my kids race motorcycles." You're living your childhood again through your kids and they become your main source. When you lose that kid or the kid moves away, you lose your source because he or she was your source for living.

There Is More

He has a blessing for every one of us. It's more than you can imagine. Many of us live in brokenness—a poverty mindset, abandonment mindset, or a fractured soul because of abuse or some other hardship.

God is willing to restore your soul man and reunite those pieces. The little chips that were broken off here and there, He wants to bring back together to make you a whole person who can move into the glory of God.

If you have a fractured piece, tell God, "I don't want that to be part of me. I bring it to You to make me whole so I can be holy because You are holy. I want to walk in the purity You have for me."

What Comes Out of Living from Your True Identity

When I was a teenager doing drugs, I would run through the streets, spray paint the back of barns, and do stupid stuff. I repented of all that. God saw that repentant heart and said, "Son, I have something for you."

He began to teach me how to live with Him at my center. He taught me how to recognize His voice and the value of obedience. God took me from level to level and taught me things in each level. He brought me through them to a place of greater healing, deliverance, and freedom.

Live Jesus

Paul tells us:

> My counsel for you is simple and straightforward: Just go ahead with what you've been given. You received Christ Jesus, the Master; **now live him**. You're deeply rooted in him. You're well constructed upon him. You know your way around the faith. Now do what you've been taught. School's out; quit studying the subject and start living it (Colossians 2:6,7, MSG, emphasis added).

I love that Paul says, "now live him." If God asks you to do something and you say yes, it means He can trust you with that yes. He wants to trust you with the yes He has for you. He has a yes for every one of us because He said yes to paying the price for you and me.

The outcome of saying yes

In Genesis 12:1-2, God told Abraham He would bless Abraham like he had never imagined. Abraham didn't know what was in front of him. His yes would birth a generation of blessings for the whole world to prepare a way for the Messiah hundreds of years later to come through another yes, the yes Mary said (see Luke 1:38). Abraham had no knowledge of the repercussions before he said yes.

Throughout the Bible, we read inspiring stories of people who said yes to God. The call and the purpose for their lives along with their obedience and surrender to God paved the way for His plan of salvation to unfold.

He's called us all here for a reason, for a purpose. It's not by happenstance. What you do with that is up to you. How you grow is up to you. If you get in the Word of God daily and stay in the Word of God, you're going to understand more and more. You will learn to not lean on your own understanding (see Proverbs 3:5), but on the very word of God so you stay centered up to reach people for heaven.

Living water

"In the last day, that great day of the feast, Jesus stood and cried, saying, 'If any man thirsts, let him come unto

Me, and drink. He who believes in Me, as the Scripture has said, out of his heart will flow rivers of living water'" (John7:37-38, NKJV).

If you're thirsty, if you need something more, Jesus invites you to come to Him and drink. You will flow with rivers of living water. If the brook inside you is dried up, drink more than a little lick of water. You need to be overflowing with water.

Because of God we can have eternal life, be fulfilled, and know our true identity. We can learn how to love, not with a tainted love we grew up with, but a true love, an actual love from heaven.

Liberty and levels

Being in the center of God's will means you perceive things differently than people who are not. When you come to that place of center beside Him, knowing what He has for you, He will make you a fisher of men. He will take you to the next level.

Stay there, find the things you struggle with, and allow God to mend those nets. When you do, He can take you to the next place He's called you to be. Jesus moves us from glory to glory, from level to level, when we are centered up with Him.

Paul tells us in 2 Corinthians 3:17, "Now the Lord is the Spirit, and where the Spirit of the Lord is, there is freedom" (NASB1995).

Where the Spirit of the Lord is, there is freedom. There is liberty. If you do not have freedom or liberty in your life, maybe you need to ask God for salvation and the Holy Spirit. If you don't know freedom and liberty in your life, you might not have taken the first step or known evidence of Holy Spirit active in your life.

We have to mend our nets by allowing God to mend the wounded places in our current level so we can move on to the next level and the next. Don't rush the glory God has for you. Find the healing in the place where you are and move on when God says to move on. If you need something more, Jesus offers it.

Paul tells us in 2 Corinthians 5:17 that we are new creations. We can break off every wrong thing that chased us and put us in a corner because we have freedom in Christ. That freedom offers another way to view identity as we will see next.

7. ANOTHER WAY TO THINK OF IDENTITY

Although we are new creations, we still carry our soul's history. Being healed of the wounds in our past can help us walk in our identity as new creations. Jesus taught by using parables, stories about common things. We can think of the car, a common thing, as an analogy for our identity.

The Car Analogy

When people talk about cars, some say the engine is the main thing because it makes the car powerful. But the engine is nothing without the wheels, which are nothing without the lug nuts to hold them in place. The lug nuts are nothing without the bolts. A car without tires won't roll.

The bumpers are for protection. The handles open the doors. The radio gives your car a voice. The starter, the fuel pump, the fuel tank are all parts of the whole thing.

You can tear apart a car and see more powerful parts. We all know this: everything must be in order for the car to operate as designed.

What shape is my car in

Your life might be like a clunky car that barely gets down the road. I call it a Rolls Canardly because it rolls down one hill and can hardly get up the next. But it won't get you there efficiently because the engine doesn't have the right tuning.

It's not functioning the way it was built to function. Barely getting down the road is not going to reach the full potential of where God called you to be.

When a car breaks down, or when we break down in our walk with God, we are not fully functioning. In this analogy, if God needs you to get somewhere in a hurry and you're driving a vehicle with a top speed of 35 miles an hour, you're not likely to arrive in time for God to minister to the people He's called you to minister to.

Staying in tune

That's why we have to make sure our car (our life) is in tune, for when we are in tune with Jesus, we operate fully. When Jesus is the center of our life, or when the yes we have for Jesus places Him at the center, then the circumference of our life will come into alignment.

Your marriage will come into alignment. Your relationships will come into alignment. Your children will come into alignment. The circumference has to come into alignment because God has centered that up once you make Him the center. He's made it that way, something like the way the universe works.

These days you can get dyno tuning for sports cars where they electronically identify ways the engine isn't running to spec. To me, dyno tuning would be like the Holy Spirit working within us. I want every glitch taken care of so I can move smoothly and quickly to the place God wants me to be.

Each person has a purpose or calling, just as each part of a car has a purpose, and we're all a part of the big plan.

Do You Know Your Calling?

As part of that big plan, God has a calling for each person. You have to grasp your identity as God sees you. What does that look like? Genesis 1:26-28 in The Message version tells us God's intention in creating us in His image. He said, "Let us make human beings in our image, make them reflecting our nature . . ." (MSG).

He's created us in His image to reflect His very nature.

Since God has a calling for each one of us, we can't think less of that calling than God thinks of it. When God gives us a call, no matter how great or small *we* think the call is, He considers the call necessary in order for each person to reach their full potential in Him.

God never makes a mistake

Some people think they are a mistake, born the wrong gender or something different from what they are. That is not true. God never makes a mistake.

Sometimes, hurt people believe they should not be here because their parents said they were a mistake and so they deny their own identity. If it's true they were a mistake, how many other people and stories and events are affected and changed by that lie?

He did not make a mistake with you, and He did not make a mistake with me. It doesn't matter how you were conceived or what happened before. Whatever bad choices people make, God never makes mistakes. He has a plan for every human on earth to know the identity He has for them.

God dreamed of you

In Ephesians 1:4, Paul tells us ". . . He chose us in Him before the foundation of the world, that we should be holy and without blame before Him in love . . ." (NASB1995). God dreamed of us before the foundation of the earth to be amazing sons and daughters. God saw us and still sees us that way.

When He dreamed of you, He dreamed you to have a mighty heart on fire, a heart true and real for God, one without mistakes because God never makes mistakes.

When you look in the mirror, you see yourself with flaws and problems. God understands how you view your current reality but He is not bound by that and neither are you. God sees you how He dreamed you to be and that's how He wants you to see yourself.

"But we all, with unveiled faces, looking as in a mirror at the glory of the Lord, are being transformed into the same image from glory to glory, just as from the Lord, the Spirit" (2 Corinthians 3:18, NASB1995).

After you choose Jesus, when you look in the mirror, you can choose to see yourself where God sees you—in the Lord Jesus Christ and in the Spirit of God. That's how He sees you. He doesn't see you confined in the mess you see.

He's going to show you how He sees you, because He sees you how He dreamed you to be. You must understand God sees you and me how He dreamed us to be.

God's thoughts toward us are peace

God wants you to have an intimate relationship with Him. He's thinking thoughts of peace for you and for me. Thoughts of peace, not of evil.

"For I know the thoughts that I think toward you, says the Lord, thoughts of peace and not of evil, to give you a future and a hope" (Jeremiah 29:11, NKJV).

If there's evil in your life or dark things, they're not coming from God. They're coming from the enemy. During dark times in my life, I looked in the mirror and I just saw ugly. I said, "Man, I don't want to look in the mirror anymore."

When the enemy tries to say you are a mistake, you have authority to beat down the lie and say, "No, I don't believe it. I do not receive it because I was made to be born into this world. I was meant to be a child of God and imitate Jesus."

Now when I look in the mirror, I no longer see a drug addict or a drug dealer or a sexist pig. I see myself the way God sees me. I've overcome past things from the world I lived in. I'm a victorious warrior and an overcomer. That's how He sees me. I'm excited about that person. When I look in the mirror, I decree the things God says about me because I belong to Him.

The cost of belonging

Jesus paid a price for us so we are not eternally separated. He paid the price of His life and His blood. When you are covered by the blood of Jesus and the enemy accuses you of doing wrong, God says, "They did what?"

He doesn't see any of it. Why? Because you're covered by the blood of Jesus. The Holy Spirit is your testimony. Psalm 103:12 tells us "As far as the east is from the west, so far has He removed our transgressions from us" (NASB1995).

Instead of being eternally separated, we eternally get to be in the light as He is in the light (see 1 John 1:7). That's what He did for you and for me.

"For it is the God who commanded light to shine out of darkness, who has shone in our hearts to give the light of the knowledge of the glory of God in the face of Jesus Christ" (2 Corinthians 4:6, NKJV).

That's you and me. Out of darkness, light will shine.

The same God shines in our hearts to illuminate us to the knowledge of the glory of God. We have to know we are children of light.

". . . for you were once darkness, but now you are light in the Lord; walk as children of light . . . " (Ephesians 5:8, NASB1995).

Children of light

We walk as children of light in this world.

"I . . . beseech you to walk worthy of the calling with which you were called . . . (Ephesians 4:1, NASB1995).

Because you said yes to Jesus, Paul tells us to imitate God. "Therefore be imitators of God as dear children" (Ephesians 5:1, NKJV).

Because you said, "God, come into my heart, live in my life," He adopted you into His kingdom. When He adopted you into His kingdom, everything that's His is yours, and everything that's yours is His.

That means we should be imitators of God because we are His children. We do like Jesus did. Is there room for selfishness and self-indulgence? Not if we want to walk as Jesus did.

Not just imitators of Jesus but identified with Him

If we are going to imitate Jesus, we're going to be identified with what He did. We're going to pay a price. We will experience difficult things.

He walked in love, all the way to the cross. He invites us to come alongside. Do what Jesus did and walk in love. You'll learn a new way to live—in freedom, our next pillar.

8. THIRD PILLAR: FREEDOM

When you got saved, Jesus freed you of all things, once and for all. From the moment you say, "God, forgive my sins and cleanse me from all unrighteousness," freedom is yours and you are a new creature. Real life kicks in at that moment and you have to start living that life. Now we have Holy Spirit inside of us.

I want to liken it to this. We broke the law by sinning. When we go to jail, we pay the price for breaking the law and it's done. That's how the law works. But Jesus came to fulfill the law by living without sin. Because He was sinless, He could pay the price for all sin for all time. Now we no longer have to pay the price. We live in grace instead.

Grace Reigns

The Apostle Paul tells us, "The Law came in so that the offense would increase; but where sin increased, grace abounded all the more, so that, as sin reigned in death, so also grace would reign through righteousness to eternal life through Jesus Christ our Lord" (Romans 5:20-21, NASB1995). The phrase "grace abounded all the more" means the price Jesus paid on the cross continues to go on and on through generation after generation, bringing freedom after freedom. Now grace reigns.

That means everything from the past is under Jesus' blood, never to be remembered against you again. It doesn't matter what you've done. Not one thing is ever remembered against you again by heaven or God. ". . . You (God) will cast all their sins into the depths of the sea" (Micah 7:19b, NASB1995).

However, the enemy will constantly bring it back to you through triggers, through things you set in front of your eyes, through things you set in your ears. That's why we need to be healed and delivered, living a life sanctified, or holy unto Him. We can learn to walk in freedom from old sin patterns.

"What shall we say then? Shall we continue in sin, that grace may abound?" (Romans 6:1, KJV). After we get saved, after all those things are wiped away, what shall we do then? Shall we continue sinning so grace may increase? No. God forbid.

When you live centered up, you don't think, "All right, God. Here we are. You saved me. All the sin and guilt is gone and I'm justified but I'm going to keep walking the old way in sin. I'm not concerned about being sanctified or consecrated."

Those two words describe life as a believer, which starts with justification.

Justification, sanctification, consecration

Justification means just as if I never sinned. After justification comes consecration and sanctification. Consecration is being set apart or centered up. Sanctification is when the desire to sin is removed.

Consecration and sanctification are a part of your walk with God. This includes everything you do after salvation and everything you have, including your body.

"And the very God of peace sanctify you wholly; and I pray God your whole spirit and soul and body be preserved blameless unto the coming of our Lord Jesus Christ" (1 Thessalonians 5:23, KJV).

That means taking everything, all the stuff you own or manage, and you say, "God, I'm consecrating everything, and I mean everything, to You. As I walk out my sanctification, You daily show me what needs to be fixed or adjusted or changed so everything is dedicated to You and I can walk in the freedom of sanctification."

"Keep company with him and learn a life of love" (Ephesians 5:2, MSG). You might own a lot of stuff, and after salvation God might tell you to get rid of all of it. I had to sell an expensive car to drive a piece of junk so I could pay my bills. But I did it. That was one way of consecrating what I had.

Hebrews 10:14 says, "For by one offering He has perfected for all time those who are sanctified" (NASB1995). He wants us to walk in the process of being sanctified. Each day I'm walking closer and closer with Him as I shed darkness.

Freedom in sanctification

As we walk out of the shadows, we walk back into the light, into the place where we started in salvation, and now we're free from all the baggage. I want to be free of all the little things holding me down. As I sit in this center place with Him, as I'm consecrated, giving everything to him, He starts showing those little things.

When I walk through the day, He lets me know what those things are. "You haven't given this thing to Me. I want your bad habits." "I want your desire to eat and be unhealthy." "I want that unbelief, too."

I want to give Him everything, all parts of me. You and I are made up of three main parts.

The flesh

In the beginning, God made man in His image with three parts to that image. Adam became a living being made of a body, soul, and spirit.

Your body is what holds your soul and your spirit. Your body will one day perish and go back into the ground. But the soul and spirit remain.

The Bible says we are to die to living from our flesh (Romans 8:13), which is living for the things of the world.

Paul said he died daily to self and the things of self (the things of the world) in order to align with what God had for him in the soul (1 Corinthians 15:31, Philippians 1:21).

"That which is born of the flesh is flesh, and that which is born of the Spirit is spirit" (John 3:6, NASB1995). When we become a Christian, we step out of fleshly relationship into a spiritual relationship with Him.

The soul: mind, will, emotions

Our soul is made up of our mind, will, and emotions. How do we get our mind in alignment with heaven?

If you daily take this Word and start eating it and studying it, you will be transformed.

"And do not be conformed to this world, but be transformed by the renewing of your mind, so that you may prove what the will of God is, that which is good and acceptable and perfect" (Romans 12:2, NASB1995).

When we renew our minds, we are transformed to the things of Christ, which is the Word of God. You renew your mind through reading and studying the Word so you can begin understanding the Word. As you start renewing your mind, Holy Spirit starts showing you how to align with Him.

The next part of the soul is your will. When your will aligns with God's will for you, it's part of eating the Word. Your will begins to align with the will of God.

Eventually, your emotions will come into check. It's okay to be emotional. God gave us those emotions and there's a time for all of those, but our emotions should not control us.

The rage or anger when you get in a fight with a loved one are emotions we should be able to control along with the words thrown back and forth. Yes, the Bible says, "Be angry, and do not sin" (Ephesians 4:26, NKJV). We should be able to control what things come out of our heart. And when ugly words come out, when you're screaming in anger, then go back and ask: "God, what is that?"

It's called carnality, which is the desire to sin. ". . . to be carnally minded is death; but to be spiritually minded is life and peace" Romans 8:6, KJV). He wants you to be free from those fits of anger.

So when your anger gets out of control, don't let shame mess you up about it. Give it to God. Ask Him what triggered it and why you did that. Get in complete alignment with Him by reading the Word, walking in His perfect will, and then your emotions will line up. We'll talk more about this in the next chapter.

The spirit

We each have a spirit, which is the true essence of who we are. Our spirit never dies. Our spirit is how we connect divinely with God. We are able to bring heaven to earth to deal with difficult things. Why? Because we're connected with God through our spirit. The Holy

Spirit lives inside us and teaches us how to live centered up.

A discussion of our spirit and the Holy Spirit within us is beyond the scope of this book. I urge you to study the Bible to learn about our spirit and the Holy Spirit. The following passages will give you a place to start. Luke 11:13, John 14:26, John 20:22, Acts 2:38, Acts 11:16, Romans 5:5, 1 Corinthians 6:19, Ephesians 1:13, 1 Thessalonians 4:8, 2 Timothy 1:14, Titus 3:5.

A Higher View

The temple had three parts, too. It had the outer court, which would be like our body. It also had the holy place, like our soul, and then the holy of holies, which is our spirit. How interesting that God said His temple is made of these three parts and we are a temple of God.

"For we are the temple of the living God" (2 Corinthians 6:16, NASB1995). And we have access to the holy place.

". . . we have confidence to enter the holy place by the blood of Jesus" (Hebrews 10:19, NASB1995).

During that era, the high priest atoned for the sins of the people by entering the Holy of Holies once a year. This space was where God appeared (see

Leviticus 16) behind a veil, or heavy curtain 40 feet tall and inches thick, because He is holy.

No one was allowed past the veil to enter that holy space except the high priest once a year. Tradition holds that a rope was tied around the high priest's ankle to drag him out if necessary.

When Jesus died, the veil was torn top to bottom (Matthew 27:51), giving us full access to heaven on earth. We can pull anything down from heaven and insert it into our life, into any situation we're going through.

Centered up for daily living

We must take in the Word of God and stay in it. I'm speaking to everyone, including myself, because emotions are not always in check.

I want you free from freak-out mode every time something comes your way. This is how we do it: get in the Word of God. If you can, sign up for a structure on reading the Word of God or for courses on studying the Word of God. Some apps let you ask questions, such as how do I prosper in my soul.

The mystery box

You're not going to get an answer for everything you ask. This is where the mystery box concept comes into play. Sometimes you have to put inexplicable things into the mystery box as an act of trust in God.

God wants to reveal things to us. "It is the glory of God to conceal a matter, But the glory of kings is to search out a matter" (Proverbs 25:2, NASB1995). In Revelation 1:6, we see Jesus ". . . hath made us kings and priests" (KJV). (See also Revelation 5:9, KJV.) Since He has made us kings, He invites us to search the things we don't know because by doing that, we get to know Him.

I believe the deeper we dig in with Him, into the Word of God, the more questions we can pull out of the mystery box as answered. Some things we can't get answered because we're not in a place we can receive the answer He has for us.

Our intent is to get our mind in alignment with His mind, get our will and everyday actions in alignment with the will God has for us that day. Just because you want to go here or there doesn't mean God wants you to go there. You must listen. If you live close to Him, if your prayer life is good, that's your connection to get in alignment.

Prayer and alignment

I have this prayer life connection with Him. The prayer line is a three-fold cord, strong like a rope you could climb up. It's not one of those little microfibers where I could only squeeze up a little prayer. We have access from heaven to earth, from earth to heaven.

I have full access to everything. Can I tap into everything I want to? No, not yet, because I'm not fully in alignment but I'm getting closer. We all get closer by centering up.

I'm working on those things by studying the Word of God, constantly being in prayer, fasting frequently, being accountable, and knowing what His will is for my life so I can stay in it.

Finding freedom

If your life's a mess, ask the Lord to show you how to align with Him. Help your soul to prosper by reading the Word of God, by getting in alignment with His will for your life, by praying, and by being in connection with other believers. Freedom comes in faithfulness to these things.

We have a prayer line that's completely open, the most powerful connection in the world. In that connection place, we find freedom, encounter God, and discover more of who He is.

As we do, we see those encounters play out in daily life.

The next chapter shares a recent day I had. The day was marked by the freedom I have to share the love of Jesus with people who needed to encounter Him.

9. WALKING IN FREEDOM

Every day we walk into the streets, there's someone there to minister to. When we walk in perfect alignment with God's will, we can minister from a place of peace so God's love reigns. Here is an example.

From A Day Living in the Center

One morning, I had the privilege to talk with a woman suffering shame, hiding in her home because of something her husband did. I offered to pray for her while she held her son and her appearance changed. I saw the load of shame lift off her. On my way home, I had the chance to bless a father and son, both in wheelchairs, who were struggling with a car situation and needed prayer.

Later that day, we went to the state fair with our granddaughter. While we were eating there, a lady went into a seizure and was locked up, couldn't move. I walked to her table to pray for her. As soon as I said the name of Jesus, her arm lifted and she grabbed my arm. I prayed for her and she was set free. As I walked away, she picked up her drink and talked to her husband with her arms in full motion.

My granddaughter wanted to know what happened and why the lady was able to move now.

On our way out of the fair, we passed a woman the Lord told me to pray for. I knelt beside her wheelchair and asked if I could pray for her. She looked ready to die with an oxygen tank in her lap. She said she was fine. Her husband came back and I asked the same of him and got the same response: she was fine and didn't need prayer. I shared a bit of my testimony (Revelation 12:11) and I watched her walls come down. She admitted she had cancer and they let me pray.

During all these moments, I was not concerned with what people would think about me. When the lady got healed right out of the seizure, I did not try to take any glory. This was about doing what God wanted done.

I want to separate myself as far from sin as I can. At the same time, I want to center myself in Jesus as much as I can so that my inside and outside match. In other words, I want my life to be Spirit-filled and Spirit-led. As we surrender to sanctification, as we are centered up in Christ, another freedom becomes available.

Freedom from a yoyo life

Another benefit to living from your identity in Christ is freedom from being controlled by your emotions and living life like a yoyo.

Jesus never let His emotions get the best of Him. Yes, He had emotions, and yes, we have emotions. But when they control us, the yoyo effect comes in and our lives sound like this: I'm happy, I'm sad. I'm happy, I'm sad. I'm rich, I'm poor. I'm rich, I'm poor. I'm just all these ins and outs, ups and downs. It's a good day, it's a bad day.

That's how some of us do life. When you get in alignment with the Word of God, you desire your will to line up with the will of God. We don't have to live like a yoyo. We have authority to drive out those thoughts and not let them come back. "Peace I leave with you; My peace I give to you; not as the world gives do I give to you. Do not let your heart be troubled, nor let it be fearful" (John 14:27, NASB1995).

The beatitudes Jesus taught in Matthew 5 give a starting place to think differently.

Authority to think a new way

"Blessed are you when people insult you and persecute you, and falsely say all kinds of evil against you because of Me" (Matthew 5:11, NASB1995).

Jesus tells us to expect insults, persecution, and lies told about us for the sake of His name. What do you do in that situation? Here is how Jesus told us to handle it.

"Rejoice and be glad, for your reward in heaven is great; for in the same way they persecuted the prophets who were before you" (Matthew 5:12, NASB1995).

Persecution is not a new thing. We need to proclaim the Word of God to change the yoyo effect in our life.

Stopping the yoyo effect

"In this you greatly rejoice, even though now for a little while, if necessary, you have been distressed by various trials" (1 Peter 1:6, NASB1995).

Sometimes even in the center of God's will, you may be distressed by various trials if necessary.

"Rejoice, and be exceeding glad: for great is your reward in heaven" (Matthew 5:12, KJV).

We must be in this center place. We need to know who we are in Christ. We belong to the King of Kings and the Lord of Lords. He is ours and we are His. When things are going exactly how He has them planned, when you're in the center of God's will, there will be trials.

But when they occur, He says to rejoice and be exceedingly glad for your reward is great for going through them from that center place. It's not always going to be comfortable.

You must be in a place of not yoyoing so you can handle it. "You will keep him in perfect peace, whose mind is stayed on You because he trusts in You" (Isaiah 26:3, NKJV).

We're not the only ones with trials and tribulations. The Bible speaks of many.

Joseph became a mighty leader. Yet, he went through many difficulties, from being thrown in a pit, to being sold as a slave, to being falsely accused, to being thrown in prison. Through all that, he still acted from his gifting. He proclaimed the Word of God and his relationship with God. Even through all that hardship, he wasn't in yoyo mode. He knew who he was and whose he was.

God brought him out and he became victorious. He interpreted the dreams of the Pharaoh and the land was fed. The nations were fed because of Joseph enduring trials and tribulation while he remained in the center place where God needed him to be.

Jesus, perfectly centered in God, didn't want to suffer crucifixion but He prayed, "Father, if You are willing, remove this cup from Me; yet not My will, but Yours be done" (Luke 22:42, NASB1995). In that center place, we have to have that mindset.

We can pray honestly. God, I don't want to go through this. If it's Your will, take it away from me. Nevertheless, not my will, God, Your will.

The impact of the soul

Our soul plays a big part in yoyo thinking. In the last chapter we saw the three parts of us: body, soul, spirit. The soul is made up of the mind, will and emotions.

When talking about the soul, we need to know we can align our soul perfectly with God. Jesus kept His mind, will, and emotions in perfect alignment so His life was never marked by yoyo thinking.

I study Scripture so it's ready inside me for any situation. That's centered up. That's having my mind in alignment with His mind.

Jesus Showed Emotions in the Bible

In John 11 we read of Lazarus' death and Jesus' tears.

Why did He weep? Because He was out of control? No, He wept because He had compassion on Mary and Martha who were crying. He didn't cry because of the situation He was entering. He knew He would raise Lazarus from the dead so He wasn't moved by loss. He knew He had the power to pull heaven down and bring life back into this man.

Jesus lived in complete alignment with the will of God for His life. ". . . whatever the Father does, these things the Son also does in like manner" (John 5:19, NASB1995). ". . . The words that I say to you I do not speak on My own initiative, but the Father abiding in Me . . ." (John 14:10, NASB1995).

Matthew 14, Mark 6, and Luke 9 tell the story of 5,000 men plus women and children who came to Jesus. When the hour was late, they were far from home and had only five loaves and two fishes to feed them all. The disciples panicked. How would they feed the crowd?

Jesus asked simply, "What do we have?" He pulled out of heaven what He needed and inserted it into the moment. Why? Because Jesus was in complete alignment with His father.

When you get in complete alignment with God, even as your soul prospers, so your health will prosper (see 3 John 1:2). We have to check ourselves. Are we in complete alignment with God?

After the feeding of the 5,000, the disciples got in a boat with Jesus, who was at peace and went to sleep. The storm started raging. The disciples were afraid they would die while Jesus was sleeping even though they saw food miraculously provided a short time before.

Jesus stood up, spoke to the storm, and the storm calmed (see Matthew 16 and Mark 8).

The disciples needed to pay a tax but had no money for it (see Matthew 17). They are again upset but Jesus sent Peter to fish and he pulled the exact amount needed from the fish's mouth. Jesus said to give to Caesar what is Caesar's and give to God what's His. Jesus the man was in perfect alignment with God.

Jesus in complete alignment

The Bible never says Jesus was sick. Why? Because He was in alignment with divinity. His soul (His mind, will, and emotions) was in complete alignment with heaven and what heaven had for Him. So He was never sick.

Do you think we could operate the way Jesus did? He did say ". . . he who believes in Me, the works that I do, he will do also; and greater works than these he will do; because I go to the Father" (John 14:12, NASB1995). Since He operated that way, we can too.

Are we in the center with God

James tells us, "Consider it all joy, my brethren, when you encounter various trials, knowing that the testing of your faith produces endurance. And let endurance have its perfect result, so that you may be perfect and complete, lacking in nothing" (James 1:2-4, NASB1995).

When our faith is tested, it produces strength. It produces the ability to carry on and keep going forward. The perfect result of enduring is that we are perfected. In the will of God, we can bear the name of Jesus and be comfortable with it.

When you're in the will of God and you go through trials, you can be a mess and life stinks but not for long because you are in the will of God.

Do you want freedom from yoyoing

Many people look good on the outside, but they're a mess on the inside and they're living in turmoil. We all want to know how to come out of the mess yoyoing makes of our lives.

The writer of Psalm 42 understood being in a mess and in despair. He asked himself, "Why are you in despair, O my soul?" (Psalm 42:11a, NASB1995).

Why are you restless? Do you know what's making you anxious, restless, struggling through life?

The psalmist continues, "Why are you in despair, O my soul? And why have you become disturbed within me? Hope in God, for I shall yet praise Him, The help of my countenance and my God" (Psalm 42:11, NASB1995).

God is the only way out of this situation. God is the only one able to help you to get in a right place with Him where your soul is not restless, you're centered in Him, and you're not yoyoing.

God's desire for us

When our emotions are inconsistent, up and down, it's because we're not doing what God has asked us to do. Our daily activities have to line up with the will of God and what He wants for our lives.

The Apostle John talks to his friend and shares his prayer for his friend. This is what he wants for him.

"Beloved, I pray that in all respects you may prosper and be in good health, just as your soul prospers" (3 John 1:2, NASB1995).

He's saying he wants us to prosper financially. He wants us to prosper in health. Here is his description of how we should prosper: "just as your soul prospers."

Jesus said if we're in complete alignment, we will prosper in our health and our finances. Are your finances a mess? If they are, are you in line with your soul? Is your soul in line with God's will?

Another way God wants us to prosper is in our encounters with Him. My early encounters with God helped set the course of my life after becoming a believer, as we'll see in the next chapter.

10. FOURTH PILLAR: ENCOUNTER

Jesus wants you to have a real encounter with Him. "Better is one day in your courts than a thousand elsewhere" (Psalm 84:10, NIV). Better is one encounter with You, God, than all the world has to offer.

We need to seek that encounter. When you see what God wants to do through that, He'll give you many more encounters. You can daily encounter Jesus.

My Early Encounters

When God began to co-labor with me, a friend and I had experiences with God our denomination didn't understand so I didn't know they were encounters. One time, Jesus came down and wrapped His arms around me. I felt like a baby mushed in the arms of God. Other times, this friend and I laughed for days until our stomachs hurt. I had out-of-body experiences.

Later, Shelly and I attended a ministry where we felt an open heaven of God's presence poured out. God was teaching us there and we saw things in the spirit.

Then God encountered me in a way that impacted the rest of my life because many of the signs came at one time. We went to a healing conference and one of the first things I saw was after the pre-service prayer time. When prayer was over, people lurched out of the prayer room. I didn't believe it was of God.

I asked Shelly, "Why are they all staggering?" She told me they were drunk in the Holy Spirit. I had no idea what that was. She explained that sometimes when people encounter the Holy Spirit, they feel as if they are drunk and may act like it.

I asked, "What do I do?"

She said, "You're just going to have to go up front to ask God." As people went up front for worship, I wedged myself between the two main speakers.

I silently prayed, God, what are You doing? The next thing I knew, I woke up reading a label on the bottom of a chair.

My skin was as red as a red shirt and I was in a daze. I got up, staggering and trying to find out what was going on, what I was going through, how I got on the floor, how I got underneath the chair. While stumbling around, I waved my arms.

As I waved one arm, people on that side of the room fell over. I looked at them and I started laughing and they started laughing. Then, I waved the other arm and the people on that side fell over. It felt like everyone in the room was focused on me. I had never known anything like this.

I wondered what this was, with people falling over. Shelly was in back waving a flag. I worked my way back to her and said, "What's going on?"

She said, "You're drunk in the Spirit."

A feather fell from somewhere, and then more feathers fell.

I asked, "What is this?"

And she said, "Grab them!" I kept reaching up, grabbing feathers out of the air.

It was the craziest experience I had ever had. This event was spectacular with all the flavors of an encounter with God.

This encounter became a turning point; I knew God is who He says He is.

Growing Spiritually

The Lord moved us on from that place of worship. He always gave us a clear heads-up on what to do. If it wasn't audible, He might as well have written out what to do. Sometimes we would lay out a fleece (see Judges 6), and He would answer through the fleece.

Shelly was going through year one of a local ministry school. She learned the concepts of the supernatural in school and I experienced it firsthand. I foresaw things. Once while I was on the phone with Shelly I had a vision of her mom coming to meet me where I was working. I said, "I just foresaw your mom coming to meet me here in Terre Haute in a little bit."

She said, "What do you mean? Why would she go to Terre Haute?"

After I hung up with her, her mom called me and said, "I'm here in Terre Haute. Where do you want to meet?"

For a while I saw captions over people's heads. It was too much for me to walk around and see information over people's heads, of their sin, of what they were doing, their lives. I just asked the Lord not to show me. I told Him it felt like a comic book thing.

Now everything is internal. God gives it to me, and I see it in my heart. I see someone, and I see things on them.

More on encounters

Encounters are real. I've had so many kinds of encounters in my life. Some have been with Father God, some have been with Holy Spirit, some have been with Jesus personally.

I've had out-of-body experiences where I was in the heavenly atmosphere watching myself doing something. My wife and I have time traveled, like Jesus did. I've heard the audible voice of God, and I've heard God in my spirit. I've heard Him speak to me and tell me to do this or do that, turn right or turn left, get up or sit down.

I told you about my time in heaven, talking face to face with Jesus. Several months later, I was driving down the road and He appeared, sitting beside me in the truck. It was so real. Jesus looked at me with that same big smile on His face. He looked at me and I started laughing. He started laughing. I called my wife and I said, "You'll never guess what happened. Jesus came to me in the truck and I was just so overwhelmed." The joy of God fell over me.

Other Encounters

God gave encounters to medical personnel who cared for me in the hospital after the wreck. While I was there those three days, when doctors or nurses walked in, I gave them prophecies and words of knowledge.

I don't remember any of it but Shelly told me afterward. I read their mail so much that some doctors changed patients because they didn't want to come in my room.

I told one doctor, "You're getting ready to change practice to Florida." He said, "How do you know that?" I said, "The Lord just told me that's what you're getting ready to do." He said, "I want to study cardiology and practice there but I haven't told people here."

A nurse was engaged to get married. I didn't know she was engaged, but when she walked in, I said, "God wants you to know the choice you're struggling with, whether this man is the right choice or not, God is saying this is the man He has for you, and it's okay to go ahead and marry."

She wept and said, "I didn't know. I've been struggling with this. How'd you know I was engaged?" I said, "The Lord showed me and wanted me to let you know."

Pastor Todd Smith, of the North Georgia Revival, had an encounter with God. He was on his knees one day, crying out to God. He looked over at the empty baptismal and saw it in a vision, full of water with fire on top. God said, "I want you to get my people in the water." Todd is a former Baptist, and he understood the significance of the water. He understood what baptism meant, but he didn't understand what God was getting ready to do. The first time they got in the water, a few people, maybe six or seven, showed up and got in the water.

They did this for a few weeks in a row, and a man got in the water with eczema all over his body. He was freshly baptized, came out of the water, and the eczema was gone. Another person got healed by getting baptized. Soon, another person got healed and another.

Pastor Todd asked, "God, what are you doing? What's going on here? We're doing baptisms. The people are getting healed." God started showing him, "I'm cleansing My bride before I come." That's what the water is all about, cleansing yourself.

Hebrew women ritually cleansed themselves before marriage or before they went to the temple and offered a sacrifice. Men also used the mikveh for cleansing. What Pastor Todd is doing is not a new baptism, but a cleansing, making you clean and whole. Since then, over 100,000 people have been healed in the waters, not just in Dawsonville, GA, but also in Martinsville, Indiana, in Illinois, in Kentucky, in other countries, from one man having one encounter with God and living out his yes to that encounter.

***

Kim Walker Smith is known for her pure expression of worship. She didn't start out that way. She experienced great emotional trauma growing up. In high school, she committed her life to God and wound up in Redding, CA. At Simpson University, she was rejected from the chapel worship team. While living in Redding, she discovered Bethel Church and decided to attend the ministry school there.

She obeyed when God told her not to sing or audition for the worship team. He wanted to heal the deep pain. The healing process took time but God brought singing back into her life and she sang on the worship team. Later she helped at a Jesus Culture conference and began to grow in her boldness and passion as a worship leader.

From there, she produced albums and traveled worldwide. Her willingness to encounter God in His way and His timing led to millions experiencing the love of Jesus through her music. We cannot count how many people have encountered God in this way.

The Next Encounter

One person, one encounter. Just imagine if you grab hold of your encounter. We understand the darker the background is, the brighter the light is. There's darkness in this life. Just stand in the light. Stand where Jesus is. Have that encounter with him.

We cannot orchestrate how our encounter with Him will be. What He requires of us is to long for and cry out to Him, to search for Him, to be willing to be a vessel of submission and honor, to be one who says, "Lord, I do want You. I want to know You better." The Lord promises if we purpose this in our heart, He will meet us in our need and encounter us.

It may not look like another's encounter, but it will be your encounter with Him. Be encouraged and long for Him and purpose in your heart, "I will love you, Lord."

As you press in to know Him, the Lord says, "I'll meet you in the secret place of prayer. I'll meet you walking on the highways and the byways. I will meet you and you will encounter Me. The encounter is available to you."

Your encounters

These are the encounters He has for you, too. He speaks to me in so many ways, and He wants that to be real in your life. He wants to speak to us in many ways, but we're dumbed down by the world and the things of the world. Some people stay in the shadows and they watch other people have the encounters.

Because some of us have not been mentored or because we are afraid of what God is going to do, we stay in these shadow places. We don't get in the center spot with Jesus where all the shadows fade and the light becomes so real, the love is so mighty.

I know what it's like to be in the center of God's will, but I also know what it's like to be in the shadows. Still being a Christian, but living somewhat of a façade, afraid to come to the center because when I get to the center place, God is going to do things that might be uncomfortable. You might be uncomfortable with some of the things God is calling you to do.

Many people don't know how to have an encounter because they're not digging deep, they're not paying the price on their knees in prayer, in the Word of God.

We must repent, believe, and receive. Will you receive what He has for you, which is a place in the center of His heart? And will you actually believe He is who He says He is and let Him have full control of your life? This is what leads to encounter.

I cannot give you my encounter. I can tell you about my encounter, but you must have your own encounter with Him. You can hear mine, and it'll push you toward wanting your own. You can almost ride the coattails of mine and glean from it. But it won't be the same.

Why? At the end, God will say, "I never knew you; depart from Me" (Luke 7:23, NKJV) because you never had an encounter with Him. We don't want man's ways and wisdom to replace God's ways and wisdom. The encounter is a big deal. You have to encounter Him.

In the next chapter, we'll discuss how to prepare yourself for encounter.

11. PREPARING FOR ENCOUNTER

I believe you want an encounter to be able to share God's love and make a difference. We can prepare for an encounter in many ways. The first one is to deal with church hurt.

Church Hurt

Many people today have been hurt by the church. I would even say everyone has church hurt and it has become a silent killer. Matthew 26 shows us an example from Jesus' time.

"At that very moment, the party of high priests and religious leaders was meeting in the chambers of the Chief Priest named Caiaphas, conspiring to seize Jesus by stealth and kill him" (Matthew 26:3, MSG).

The church leaders of the day plotted to have Jesus killed by the region's governing authorities. Believers who live their lives centered up in Jesus do at times hurt people. This is not malicious but just a natural outcome of living for Jesus in a messed-up world and right overcoming wrong.

Caiphas, the chief priests, and the elders delivered Jesus to Pontius Pilate the governor. This was the time of year when Pilate released one prisoner. However, he saw no wrong in Jesus so he offered the people a choice of who to release.

"The governor . . . said to them, 'Which of the two do you want me to release to you?' They said, 'Barabbas!'" (Matthew 27:21, NKJV).

Barabbas was a known murderer but these church leaders feared a riot and didn't want to hurt anyone's feelings. When we live in line with Jesus, we'll step on toes and offend people because of the Word we carry. The gospel is always going to stir up some stuff.

"Pilate said to them, 'What then shall I do with Jesus who is called Christ?'" (Matthew 27:22, NKJV). He was talking about the one who raised the dead and healed people.

The multitude, some who were fed miraculously, and some who laid down cloaks, shouting "Hosanna"— how did they answer?

"They all said to him, 'Let Him be crucified!'" (Matthew 27:22, NKJV).

The Christian who doesn't live centered up with Jesus is doing the same thing as those who said crucify Him.

Living centered up

Going to church on Sunday morning is important but it does not make you centered. Only you and Jesus can do that.

Even when we live centered up, we still get hurt. How did Jesus handle this? In the worst pain and humiliation, He said, "Father, forgive them, for they do not know what they do" (Luke 23:34, NKJV). This includes the ones going to bars on the weekend or looking at things they're not supposed to see, the ones abusing others, beating others, slandering others, cheating others.

Do we say "Father, forgive them" about these who have hurt us? I do not hold grudges against anybody. When I was beaten black and blue from the back of my leg all the way to the top of my shoulders, my whole back was purple. I forgave almost immediately when I was abused in any way you can imagine. I forgave and I still forgive. I can be around those people all day long, and it doesn't bother me.

How are you forgiving today

Can we forgive like Jesus forgave? God is looking for
an army that bears good fruit and loves unconditionally.
If you want to know how to live, study the book of John.
If you do not read the Bible at all, get in the book of
John and read it through. If you read it through and read
it through, He will show you examples of love and
forgiveness and kindness and purity and
wholesomeness.

The book of John was my dad's favorite book. I
didn't know it till I went to his funeral. I found out his
favorite verse was John 14:6, which is my favorite
verse. I never received ministry from my dad, but he
ministered to hundreds of men.

If you didn't have your dad in your whole life, and
when you go to the funeral and discover he ministered
to all these other men and boys but not you, if your
heart's not positioned right, you would feel like, wow,
what about me? But I could say, "God, thank You that
he got to minister to all those men." I was excited my
dad got to touch the lives of so many. Even though I
was hurt by our fractured relationship, I still forgave him.

Forgiveness is not a feeling but a choice. It doesn't
mean the person you forgive is free to continue bad

behavior toward you. It doesn't mean you forget those behaviors. Forgiveness is giving up your right to "justice" as we define it. And forgiveness often is a process of choosing to extend grace repeatedly for your mental and spiritual benefit.

Poor choices

As I travel for ministry, I see people, even pastors, doing things that get in the way of being centered up with Jesus. Many people are messed up because they are not in a center place with God. They let church hurt determine their lives.

The enemy's trying to pull you away from your destiny. Most people are in a jail of some kind because their identity isn't the way God designed it. People who have been in the church and walked away from the church go back into those comfort zones where they used to be. God has so much more for them, and He has so much more for you.

"Fake it 'til you make it"

"Better is one day in your courts than a thousand elsewhere" (Psalm 84:10, NIV).

I've seen people on the outside of His courts. I've been to a lot of churches and seen many fake encounters because the enemy lied to people and told them to fake it until they make it.

If we see someone acting out an encounter, we have a choice. We can check in with God to ask if what they're doing lines up with Scripture, if it lines up with the context of the meeting, if internally Holy Spirit is asking anything of us in response.

"As iron sharpens iron, So one person sharpens another" (Proverbs 27:17, NASB1995). If we're part of this body, we're supposed to sharpen one another in love.

It takes time to grow in discernment. We have to learn what a real encounter is. When we do, we become like the Book of Acts and we get in one accord. What happens? The fire falls; heaven falls and resonates in our spirits.

Parable of the Ten Virgins

The parable of the virgins provides another perspective on encounters. While Jesus was here, He told a story to the people using familiar cultural events.

> Then the kingdom of heaven shall be likened to ten virgins who took their lamps and went out to meet the bridegroom. Now

five of them were wise, and five were foolish. Those who were foolish took their lamps and took no oil with them, but the wise took oil in their vessels with their lamps. But while the bridegroom was delayed, they all slumbered and slept.

And at midnight a cry was heard: "Behold, the bridegroom is coming; go out to meet him!" Then all those virgins arose and trimmed their lamps. And the foolish said to the wise, "Give us some of your oil, for our lamps are going out." But the wise answered, saying, "No, lest there should not be enough for us and you; but go rather to those who sell, and buy for yourselves." And while they went to buy, the bridegroom came, and those who were ready went in with him to the wedding; and the door was shut.

Afterward the other virgins came also, saying, "Lord, Lord, open to us!" But he answered and said, "Assuredly, I say to you, I do not know you."

Watch therefore, for you know neither the day nor the hour in which the Son of Man is coming (Matthew 25:1-13, NKJV).

The bridegroom represents Jesus Christ. The parable is talking about His return. According to verse 13, we don't know when He will return.

The Bible talks about God as bridegroom. In the Old Testament, God is pictured as the husband of Israel in Isaiah 54:4-6, in Isaiah 62:4-5, and in Hosea 2:19. In the New Testament we see Jesus as the bridegroom in John 3:27-30, in Matthew 9:15, in Mark 19:20.

This parable relates a familiar event—the bridegroom coming for his bride. In Ephesians 2:25-32, the church is considered the bride and she is to be pure and spotless.

A western understanding of the word virgin can be limited. In the Word, virgin means to be pure. A man can be pure. A woman can be pure. Your heart can be pure. It's talking about the purity of the bride.

The oil in the parable represents the Word of God. All of us, as the church, as the bride of Christ, have access to the Word of God. We all have access to the oil that's represented with these lamps.

The extra oil the wise virgins carried with them represents the Holy Spirit. It represents an extra measure of faith and testimony through Holy Spirit living in our lives.

Jesus said, "Except a man be born of water and of the Spirit, he cannot enter into the kingdom of God" (John 3:5, KJV). We've all been born of water, natural human birth. Now He's saying we must have the Spirit, that extra oil.

We all have access to this oil, but we must have the extra oil to do what we need to do extra. The wise virgins were prepared to do more by having extra oil.

The foolish virgins were not prepared. Some people who attend church are sluggish and unprepared. They once rode on someone else's encounter with God and they had a little savor so they could minister to some people, but didn't have their own encounter.

Your own encounter means more salt

"You are the salt of the earth; but if the salt has become tasteless, how can it be made salty again? It is no longer good for anything, except to be thrown out and trampled under foot by men" (Matthew 5:13-14, NASB1995).

This passage says if you have become tasteless, you can't be made salty again. Let's consider the lack of salt or savor and the lack of oil by the foolish virgins.

If you're going on a long trip and you take only the oil in your lamp, the trip might last a little longer than you expected. If you didn't bring enough oil, your lamp is going to burn out and you're not going to have enough light.

The wise brought their lamp full of oil. Then, they had extra oil for when the lamp started getting empty. They had more oil because they brought more of Holy Spirit.

The bridegroom delayed his coming, so they were all sleeping. It was okay in that culture to sleep. In our time, it's okay to have things. It's okay to have fun. It's okay to enjoy things in the world so long as that is not what defines us.

When we deeply know the One who defines us, we live with the confidence that when we walk in a room, something happens. Something has to happen because we're there. Why? Because He's here in us. Holy Spirit lives in us and flows out of us. Our salt tastes really good. It's very flavorful, not lacking anything.

They were all sleeping. Some of the church is sleeping and not cultivating their salt by spending time with Holy Spirit. Some who call themselves believers choose behavior that is not like Jesus.

Back then, the household had their lamps going because the bridegroom would come in the night hour to the bride's house. The bride's maids were supposed to light the way for the bridegroom to come to the house of the bride. These 10 virgins were probably the bride's maids. The lord of the house, that is, the father of the bride, would open the doors and let everybody in.

In this story, the 10 virgins were sleeping, and all of a sudden, they heard the sound. He's coming. He's coming. Wake up.

They have to light the way for the bridegroom to come down the path to the bride's house. They trim their lamps but their lamps were burning low.

Five foolish virgins without extra oil said, "Give us some of your oil." The other five said, "We can't."

In the same way, we can't give our Holy Spirit encounters to another person. It's impossible for me to give you my encounter. I can tell you about my encounter. I can tell you what Holy Spirit does in me, how He flows through me, but I can't give that encounter to you. You have to have your own encounter.

And the wise five said, "Go to the city and buy for yourselves." It was late at night and no one was open to buy from. When they came back to the house, the others were already inside and the bride's father had shut the door.

The five virgins came back from town and banged on the door to get inside. He answered, "No, I don't know who you are."

A lot of doors in the Bible have been shut

The lord of the bridal house shut the door and God shut the door to the ark. People banged on the ark. "Let us in." Noah had warned them before God shut the door. Now it was too late.

We must understand He is the one who will shut the door, just like the bride's father shut the door. Once they shut the door, all who were invited were inside.

"I never knew you. Depart from Me." Those are hard words for us to hear, to consider that our God in heaven would say, "Depart from Me, I never knew you." But it's because He never knew you.

He didn't know these five foolish ones because they were riding on someone else's encounter. They didn't have the extra oil of Holy Spirit. You can't give your encounter to someone else. You can only tell them about it.

Your own measure of Holy Spirit

Does that mean you have to speak in tongues? Absolutely not. Does it mean you're capable of speaking in tongues? Yes, it does. We have to understand what it means to have Holy Spirit in our lives.

Jesus left this world and sits at the right hand of God. Jesus said He had to go so Holy Spirit could come (see John 14:23ff) and Holy Spirit came down.

Aren't you grateful Holy Spirit came so you can have an audience with Him because He lives in you. You're able to commune with Him 24/7.

Otherwise, you would have heard about Jesus being some place on the earth and you would try to get in line to go see Him. But other people need healing. You just want to get in and talk to Him, but you wouldn't be able to get past the crowds because everybody would want to see the miracles and talk with Him.

That's one reason Jesus had to go and Holy Spirit came. Another reason is we have to be born of spirit as well as water.

It was critically important for Holy Spirit to come and it's even more important that Holy Spirit lives inside of you. This is how you become a wise child of God. You take Holy Spirit inside of you and get plugged in to the things God is doing. That's called being a wise virgin and that's when encounters happen.

The fruit of encounters

All the pillars we've discussed are interwoven and work together. When you experience life and learn your identity, when you gain freedom and have your own history of encounters with God, they lead you into the next season of your life. You get to participate in His purpose for you here on earth and make a difference in the lives of others by your yes. What happens when we live out our yes?

12. MAKING MY YES COUNT

When I spoke with Jesus in heaven, I wanted to stay in heaven but I made a choice to return for my loved ones. The choice I made has impacted not only my life, but the lives of countless others. My yes matters.

My yes means I talk to people daily, one at a time or in crowds, and share the love of Jesus with them. My yes means people's lives are changed. My yes means I get to bless God with my obedience.

We all need to be molded by obedience.

Remolded By the Potter

Another way God helps us into the center place is molding us like clay on a potter's wheel. Jeremiah had an encounter with the potter to see God in this way.

> The word which came to Jeremiah from the Lord saying, "Arise and go down to the potter's house, and there I will announce My words to you." Then I went down to the

potter's house, and there he was, making something on the wheel. But the vessel that he was making of clay was spoiled in the hand of the potter; so he remade it into another vessel, as it pleased the potter to make.

Then the word of the Lord came to me saying, "Can I not, O house of Israel, deal with you as this potter does?" declares the Lord. "Behold, like the clay in the potter's hand, so are you in My hand, O house of Israel" (Jeremiah 18:1-6, NASB1995).

Can God not do the same thing with you? Can He remake you, mold you, and shape you into who He's created you to be, who He dreamed before the foundations of the earth you would be? I speak that over you in Jesus' name.

The master potter at work

I had the privilege to see a lady working with a potter's wheel. She was turning clay on the wheel and I watched how she worked. It was so cool because her hands were wet and she was getting all messy. But she was making a beautiful vessel.

While she was turning the wheel and shaping a pot, I asked, "Hey, can I do that?" If I want to do something, I'll just ask. She looked at me and I said, "I'd like to do it." She asked, "You think you could do it?" I said, "Man, I built a church. I could do something on the wheel like that." She let me.

She crushed her clay down into a ball. Then she brought me to the wheel and got my hands wet. I thought, I can do anything. But she gave me instructions. She said, "You take the clay and you knead it. Then, you throw it right in the middle of the wheel."

The importance of centering

There's the key. I threw the lump of clay on the wheel, but it was off center. When the wheel started turning, the blob of clay wobbled. The wheel turned but I could not shape the clay while it was off center. I was forced into trying to get the clay back in center.

Can you imagine? When you get saved, you automatically go to that center place because you're right there with Jesus.

As I tried to shape something on the wheel, the clay started sliding over to the side. Sometimes when we're in this center place, after we get saved and everything feels really good, we may want to start going back to our old ways. We start getting off center, and God says, "I need you in this center place."

He's trying to work with you. But when you get out of center, you're going after your will. He won't override your will. He's going to let you go your own way. He will never give up on you but He does respect your choice.

So as I was trying to get the lump of clay back in center, she said, "You've got to throw hard." I was trying to work like she did, but I had to start over and throw it back in the center place.

Finally, I got it centered. Then she told me how to form a vessel by pressing down the middle and pulling up the sides. I tried but she said, "You can't press down too hard and you can't pull up too fast." There I was, trying to push down and bring it up. The vessel began to form and I thought, "I'm making something good!" Then, all of a sudden, it went wrong again.

The master's hands

She took over. The master's hands started working. She grabbed the clay and started making this beautiful vase out of something I trashed. God wants to do that in you. God is a God of new beginnings. He wants to do something in you you've never had.

God wants to fill you full of oil. But a lot of times, we empty out because we're not healed. The vessel we're operating with has not been fully healed from wounds and cracks.

When you come into that center place with God, you build relationship with Holy Spirit. If you don't have relationship with Holy Spirit, you need one. As your relationship with Holy Spirit develops and healing comes, you hear His voice more often.

What Is Your Choice

It's a powerful thing for God to speak to us personally. When He does, we hear better what He's saying and do it. This especially applies when we call it out. We say things like, "God said to do this. God said to go there." But we don't always obey.

Disobedience has consequences.

Adam and Eve had perfect peace, perfect everything. They needed nothing. But somehow the enemy came in and deceived them. This one lie changed life for the whole world.

Shifting outside of the presence or the spirit of God has a consequence. Walking outside of the will of God (not staying centered up) is walking in the way of the world. It's just like walking in sin again.

We need to assess the damage sin has caused in our lives and to our family. Our sin has consequences that spread out from our family into our community and from there into the world. We see so much destruction in the world today.

I choose life. I understand all have sinned and fall short of the glory of God (Romans 3:23). But Jesus paid the ultimate price and redeemed us. How did we get to this destructive place?

Let someone disciple or mentor you so you can walk in the fullness of God. You will know how much darkness He brought you out of and be excited for where He is leading you.

What God wants for us

We must understand the power God has for each of us to stand up and be righteous and holy and purified.

"Call to Me and I will answer you, and I will tell you great and mighty things, which you do not know" (Jeremiah 33:3, NASB1995).

This is what God wants for you and me. But if you don't even know the basics in the Word of God, He cannot give you this kind of information. It will mess you up.

People don't understand the basics of what they're supposed to know as believers.

He talks about time travel and going from here to there in a moment, angels in the room. Those things do happen.

But if you're an uneducated Christian, you'll come into a church-type setting and say, "Oh, they're talking about angels." And that's all you will leave with. Why? Because you have not let the Word of God change you.

Purifying is required

"Many will be purged, purified and refined, but the wicked will act wickedly; and none of the wicked will understand, but those who have insight will understand" (Daniel 12:10, NASB1995).

Holy Spirit lives inside of me. He wants to live inside of you and teach you so the Word of God changes you. You must be pure to have the clearance to see the things He wants to show you.

We can think of purification like a series of filters. The first filter lets through everything in your life except the biggest junk. Holy Spirit will come alongside and ask if you will let go of the thing that is not part of the Kingdom of God. He asks for our benefit, not His.

Then, He will bring in the next level of filter to address the next size of things to be purified or filtered out of your life. Each filter gets finer to refine your life from all the things not of Him.

Being filtered

When I got saved, I had a lot of junk in my life. Then as I got walking with Him, I started reading the Bible and studying the Word of God. I started learning about Him and who He is, learning who I am, my identity. Then, He started to ask if I would let go of a little bit more.

He said, "I want this, this, this and this. I want these things out of your life now. You've come this far and you've got the clearance to get to this place if you'll let Me refine you."

There's still some stuff in me. I'm going to shake the things that are not part of the Kingdom of God because I know I'm not going to be 100% until I step into heaven, but I know I could be 99.9%.

The Apostle Paul

Paul was a man who went out and killed Christians (see Acts 9). But Paul is not known for that because God remolded him. Remember, Paul went from Saul to Paul, killing Christians, and God stopped him in his tracks. Why?

Because God didn't create him or dream Paul's life to destroy Christians. God stopped him and said, "Why are you persecuting Me?" God healed his wounds.

I know his wounds were healed because Paul always glorified God even though he went through many trials. He was in and out of prisons, shipwrecked, but he never once said a negative thing to God. He glorified God, where he was, whatever he was doing, whatever situation he was in.

That's being in the center place. God remolded Paul to become a mighty man of God.

I've touched on many large concepts in this book. If you encountered things you don't understand, check the Resources page where you can learn how to contact me or to start studying with Kineo.

Making My Yes Count

I don't claim to be on Paul's level but my yes makes a difference. Each day I live centered up and because of that, people get to choose their own yes.

I was released from the hospital on the third day after the accident and my yes continued.

After I went home, I slept something like 20 hours a day. A week later, I had a stroke. It caused me to lose my speech—I knew what I wanted to say but couldn't string the words together.

I went to my family doctor, who ordered another MRI and confirmed I had a severe stroke. He said it could be months, if not years, before I got my speech back because of how bad the stroke was.

I got tired of being home in bed and needed to get out of the house, once my body was up to it. A friend invited me to play disc golf. I couldn't play, but I wanted to go with him. While he was playing, he offered to pray for me. That night I felt heat in my stomach. After I went to bed, I woke up and started praying in the spirit.

I can talk

Shelly woke up, and she heard me praying out loud. I said, "I can talk now."

Soon my family doctor called the house and said, "I need to speak with Jason." I said, "This is Jason." He said, "No, Jason Abney." I said, "This is Jason." He asked, "Well, what happened to make you talk?" I said, "God healed me." He responded, "I've got to see you." So we went to see him.

He could not understand how I regained my speech and ordered another MRI.

We went to see him afterward and he showed us the MRIs taken at the hospital after the accident when they told us about the brain trauma. "You've got all this brain trauma from the accident; the MRI shows the brain trauma is severe. It's everywhere, all over the scans."

Then he showed the one taken after the stroke which showed the damage from the stroke and pointed out that damage.

Then he put up the last one and said, "There's no brain trauma here. It doesn't show anything. I see a little scar on the brain, but that had to be from when you were a little boy, maybe seven or eight." When I was eight, I had a wreck on my bicycle. Other than the boyhood scar, no trauma showed in the most recent MRI.

Then came TMJ

Later, I went to the dental school, first for teeth broken in the wreck, and later for TMJ. When I went back for the TMJ, he said because of how the wreck injured my mouth, he would have to do surgery and wire my jaw shut for several weeks.

That Friday, my jaw locked shut on its own. I could not move my mouth. Sunday we went to church, and some women prayed for me. On the third day, my jaw popped open, and the TMJ was gone. I went back to the doctor and they did more scans. He said, "You don't have TMJ. What happened?" I said, "God healed me." This guy was amazed.

Knee injury

I also had a torn meniscus in my knee. It was a one-inch tear from the way my leg had twisted in the wreck. The medical people said it would require surgery and I would be down for six months or so. Someone at church prayed for my meniscus. On the third day after prayer, I went to this surgeon and he confirmed a one-inch tear on the hospital MRI. He said, "We're going to have to go in here to put that back together."

I said, "No. God has healed me. The tear is not there anymore." He mocked me, saying, "Yeah, okay." He put me on the table, started manipulating my leg, and he bent my leg all the way to my chest. He watched my face, and asked, "Does that hurt?" I said, "No. I told you, God healed me."

Bills paid

The medical bills were huge and we didn't have health insurance, only full-coverage auto.

Soon after I arrived at the hospital, a girl named Jasmine came in the room and said, "Hey, when you came in, I saw there was no insurance. I just want you to know I paid $10 out of my pocket to get you enrolled in this plan for people who don't have insurance."

Shelly called after the accident to learn more from Jasmine about how all this worked. She told Shelly, "Call me back around Thanksgiving" since it takes a while for all the bills to come in.

Somehow, the insurance was in effect. We don't know if it was because she bought it before all the diagnoses were rolled out. Later Shelly tried to reach Jasmine but was told each time no Jasmine worked there.

We don't know if this person was a human or an angel.

Our auto insurance was full coverage so we had a payout there. The insurance Jasmine bought for me while I was in the hospital paid a lot, but after all insurance payouts, we still had over $100,000 in bills for those three days.

Months later the hospital called and said, "We've written off every bill. You owe us nothing." Later, all the doctors called and said they had written off all their bills as well.

Everything was erased from the wreck except the scars. I believe my yes played a part in the new healings and in clearing the debts.

The Importance of Your Yes

You might be wondering why I included the story of Jesus saying yes to me. The reason it is so important is that I said yes to Him. My yes changed the future, not just for me, but for many people. The same is true for you and your yes.

My decision of whether to say yes has eternal consequences and so does your decision.

When I stay centered up in God, I encounter people every day who need to know Him. They also get the choice to say yes to Jesus and to heaven.

This is why your yes matters. Each day we encounter people who need to know that any bad thing in their lives can be overcome by the blood of the Lamb.

If we have not said yes to Jesus and to staying centered up in Him, people may miss heaven. Your yes matters.

MY PRAYER

Lord, take me to the center place that lines up with You, the place where You are all I need. And Lord, take me high enough to kill all my desires for the world and the things in it. Take me deep enough in You, Lord, to suffocate the things that are not of You. Take me to the place You dreamed for me before the world began.

Help me learn to say yes to You and all You have for me, yes to all of Your plans, yes to Your blessings, to the peace You have for me. Father, help me say yes to the Love, to the Identity, to the Freedom, to the Encounters heaven has for me until the day we meet face to face for that final call.

Show me the multitude You have for me. I choose to be in alignment with You to serve them and bring them to You that not one is missed.

I pray this prayer in Jesus' name, the name above all names.

ABOUT AUTHOR

Jason Abney and his wife Shelly pastor Life of Love
Ministry Center in Martinsville, IN. Jason and Shelly
have five sons and 12 grandchildren.

Jason grew up in sometimes life-threatening
circumstances but God graciously encountered Jason
at the age of 8 through the TV ministry of Billy Graham.
Jason's circumstances didn't change for many years but
he was radically redeemed from drug addiction. He
went on to work in construction and then law
enforcement. Later he returned to construction while
bounty hunting, which he did for two years with 218
captures. Jason left bounty hunting to serve God full
time as a pastor.

Besides taking an active part in their community, they have seen thousands healed in the waters of baptism over the last several years. Regular water immersion services in their ministry center resulted from meeting Dr. Todd Smith at the North Georgia Revival.

Jason and Shelly live to represent Jesus to everyone they meet and to reach others with the love of Jesus.

If you need help, a great place to start is the Resources page.

Another great resource is yesministries.lol

RESOURCES

Locally

Being part of a local, vibrant church body is essential to your spiritual health. If you struggle to find a place to worship in person, ask Holy Spirit to lead you. Also ask friends, family, and social media. Consider how far you are willing to drive on a regular basis—it could be worth more than you know.

To request prayer or ask questions

Complete the Prayer Request Link on the Life of Love website at https://lol-mc.com/ You can reach Pastor Jason by text only at 812-241-1395.

Kineo Ministry Training Center — https://kineomtc.com

For study of the Word: Kineo Ministry Training Center moves students forward in their relationship with God, in their knowledge of the Word, and in their preparation to minister to others. Students will be made ready to give an answer, a reason, for their hope in Jesus Christ (1 Peter 3:15) and more capable and confident in bringing others into this same hope (2 Corinthians 5:20).

Kineo Kids (https://kineokids.com/) is not your typical Bible study for children. Kineo Kids dive into the Word of God and discover the wonder and joy of Jesus as seen on every page! Designed for students 3rd grade and up.

Todd Smith —
https://lifeinchristchurch.cc/media/speaker/Pastor+
Todd+Smith

Selected titles:

- *Speaking in Tongues: Your Secret Weapon*
- *Unless We Pray: The Hour is Late. God has a Plan and This is It!*
- *Igniting Revival Fire Everyday: 70 Invitations that Awaken Your Heart from Global Revivalists*
- *40 Days: A Journey Toward a Deeper Relationship with Christ*
- *He Sat Down*
- *He Sent Him: Understanding and Releasing the Power of the Holy Spirit in Your Life*

- *Come Alive Dry Bones: The Pathway to the Next Great Awakening*

Roberts Liardon — https://www.robertsliardon.org

Selected titles:

- *Mantles Past and Present: What Mantles Are and How They Work*
- *God's Generals: Why They Succeeded and Why Some Failed*
- *Smith Wigglesworth: The Complete Collection of His Life Teachings*
- *Why the Devil Doesn't Want You to Pray in Tongues*
- *Maria Woodworth-Etter: The Complete Collection of Her Life Teachings*
- *Kathryn Kuhlman: A Spiritual Biography of God's Miracle Worker*
- *Sharpen Your Discernment: Because When Life Looks Grey, It's Really Black & White*

Larry Arendas

- *Stuck*
- *Song of the Dinosaurs*
- *Set the Captives Free Manual*
- *Commentary on the Gospel of Matthew*
- *You and God*
- *The Theology of Baseball*

Derrick Snodgrass

- *Sons of Purpose, a View of Biblical Heroes through the Eyes of 21st Century Men: a 40 Writer Collaboration*
- *The Supernatural Power of Fasting: Turning Our Hearts Back to the Father*
- *The Supernatural Power of Tears: Turning Our Hearts Back to the Father*

David Edmondson, Marty Darracott

- *The Man In The Office Next Door*

David Edmondson

- *The Joshua Generation*
- *The Prodigal Father*
- *The Forming Process*

Lance Johnson

- *Revival: The Coming Storm*
- *Revamp: The Pathway To Recovery*

Marty Darracott

- *Echo Heaven: Secrets to Hearing God's Voice and Receiving Words of Knowledge*

David Hayes — https://prayingmedic.com/

Dave was an atheist, serving as an EMT and paramedic for 35 years. In 2008, God appeared to Dave in a dream and said He would heal Dave's patients if he prayed for them. Dave didn't believe in healing at the time, but reluctantly began praying. He had no idea what he was doing, but along the way, he stumbled upon some keys to operating in healing and miracles. He produces books, podcasts, and online classes.

Selected titles:

- *Emotional Healing Made Simple*
- *Dream Interpretation Made Simple*
- *Power and Authority Made Simple*
- *Divine Healing Made Simple*
- *Hearing God's Voice Made Simple*
- *Seeing in the Spirit Made Simple*
- *Traveling in the Spirit Made Simple*

ACKNOWLEDGEMENTS

I want to thank my wife Shelly for all she is. I am privileged to love her. She has been a pivotal part of my life and ministry. I understand the Holy Spirit so well because of her and that makes all the difference. I would not be the man of God I am today without her. She has graciously put up with my shenanigans while writing this book and loves me anyway.

I met Pastors Todd and Karen Smith in Georgia at the North Georgia Revival. They are warm, compassionate people. Their mentoring has been key to my growth and their help and friendship is the reason this book happened.

I also want to thank Rachel Hills of https://authorswhoserve.com/ for her coaching and editing of this book. Writing a book is a huge project and she is knowledgeable about the entire process. Whatever help I needed, she came through. I can't thank her enough for her patience in walking me through this demanding but rewarding endeavor.

www.ingramcontent.com/pod-product-compliance
Lightning Source LLC
Chambersburg PA
CBHW061756120626
46550CB00005B/2021